FAMILIES

OF ADULTS

WITH

AUTISM

FAMILIES

OF ADULTS

WITH

AUTISM

Stories and Advice for the Next Generation

Edited by *Jane Johnson* and *Anne Van Rensselaer*

Foreword by *Stephen M. Edelson*, Ph.D.,
Director of the Autism Research Institute, USA

Jessica Kingsley Publishers
London and Philadelphia

First published in 2008
by Jessica Kingsley Publishers
116 Pentonville Road
London N1 9JB, UK
and
400 Market Street, Suite 400
Philadelphia, PA 19106, USA

www.jkp.com

Library of Congress Cataloging in Publication Data
Families of adults with autism : stories and advice for the next generation / edited by Jane Johnson and Anne Van Rensselaer ; foreword by Stephen M. Edelson. -- 1st American pbk. ed.
p. cm.
ISBN 978-1-84310-885-6 (pb : alk. paper) 1. Autism. I. Johnson, Jane, 1966- II. Van Rensselaer, Anne.
RC553.A88F36 2008
616.85'882--dc22

2007031526

British Library Cataloguing in Publication Data
A CIP catalogue record for this book is available from the British Library

ISBN 978 1 84310 885 6

Printed and bound in the United States by
Thomson-Shore, Inc.

Think of me as your future. I am where you will be many years from now, when you know how it all played out and "what will be" has turned into "what was."

And you will have come to terms with it, not perhaps in the way you thought you would, but you'll no longer feel trapped in a morass of angst and guilt. You will have resolved your child's future and your own. You'll know you've given full measure and the measure you've given has never been pointless.

Eustacia Cutler, mother of Temple Grandin
(From *A Thorn in My Pocket; Temple Grandin's Mother Tells the Family Story*, by Eustacia Cutler)

Contents

Foreword, by Dr. Stephen M. Edelson   11

Chapter 1   Helen Landalf   15

Chapter 2   Joan H. Goble, MD   22

Chapter 3   Jean and Michael Curtin   24

Chapter 4   Katie Dolan   31

Chapter 5   John Henley   33

Chapter 6   Gerda McCarthy   38

Chapter 7   Toby Arenberg   41

Chapter 8   Raymond Gallup   44

Chapter 9   Julie Gallup   48

Chapter 10   Clara Claiborne Park   50

Chapter 11   Carol Croke   53

Chapter 12   Matthew DeLuca   56

Chapter 13   Jinny and Bill Kemmel   58

Chapter 14   Elaine Woodruff   63

Chapter 15   Ann Laferty-Snowhook   66

Chapter 16   Jordan Snowhook   71

Chapter 17   Elizabeth Snowhook   72

Chapter 18   Kim Oakley   73

Chapter 19   Irina Lobkovitz   88

Chapter 20 Kristin Zhivago   92

Chapter 21 Sue Swezey   95

Chapter 22 Edith P. Gray   114

Chapter 23 Beth Sposato   117

Chapter 24 Sharon Lettick Crotzer   129

Chapter 25 Ruth C. Sullivan   133

Chapter 26 Toshiko Lyons   137

Chapter 27 Sally Graham   144

Chapter 28 Lawrence Stream   146

Chapter 29 Maxine Richards   152

Chapter 30 Arlene J. Paster   155

Chapter 31 Mary Laird Flanagan   158

Chapter 32 Dr. and Mrs. William K. Henry   161

Chapter 33 Francine M. Bernstein   166

Chapter 34 Dorothy Beavers   173

Chapter 35 Jim Cockey   178

Chapter 36 Audrey Flack   187

This book is dedicated to our hero,
Bernie Rimland.

Foreword

This book began when Bernard Rimland and I spent an evening discussing the problems faced by adults with autism, and by their families. We talked about how the generation of parents who rebelled against the "Refrigerator Mother" theory of autism, and later battled for their children's right to public education, are the same parents who blazed the trail for adult issues such as living arrangements, employment, and recreation.

We realized there was no forum where parents who'd seen their children with autism through to adulthood could share their thoughts and advice. To help correct this, Dr. Rimland and I decided to ask some families of adults with autism to describe their journey in writing. Finding our writers was a simple task, because soon after Dr. Rimland's groundbreaking book *Infantile Autism: The Syndrome and Its Implications for a Neural Theory of Behavior* was published in 1964, parents around the country began writing to him about their experiences. Over the years to follow, he kept in contact with many of them. I'd worked closely with many parents during my 30-plus years in the field as well, so it was easy for us to find candidate families in our databases, and we invited some of them to write something for the book.

You may recognize the names of some of the contributors to the book. In varying ways, all of them have been movers and shakers in the autism world. Dr. Ruth Sullivan is one of the true pioneers in the field of autism; as the first president of the Autism Society of America, she contributed significantly to our understanding of the needs of adults and the importance of adult services. Clara Park wrote one of the most popular autobiographical books on autism, *The Siege: A Family's Journey Into the World of an Autistic Child.* As a special bonus, Dr. Rimland's daughter, Helen Landalf, wrote a beautiful chapter about her brother, Mark.

Mark Rimland was the driving force behind his father's commitment to improving the lives of children and adults with autism. One of Mark's breakthroughs occurred because his father visited Dr. Ivar Lovaas at an autism research clinic at UCLA. Dr. Rimland was impressed with Dr. Lovaas's results, and quickly learned to apply the techniques to Mark's behaviors, with immediate results. Dr. Rimland started the Autism Society of America, primarily to promote the use of behavior modification. Later, realizing the critical need for effective biomedical interventions, he formed The Autism Research Institute (ARI) to further research into the causes and medical treatment of autism spectrum disorders. In the 1990s he launched the Defeat Autism Now! (DAN!) Project, revolutionizing the treatment of autistic children worldwide.

Dr. Rimland's prominence in the field of autism never distracted him from his efforts to prepare Mark for the future. Dr. Rimland very much wanted Mark to fit into society. (For instance, he made sure Mark stood straight, had a firm handshake, and was polite to everyone.)

Today, Mark is one of my closest friends. He's one year older than me, and we often go out for coffee and sometimes for a bite to eat. I've known him for about thirty years, and every year he becomes more perceptive and cognizant of his social surroundings. As many of you know, he's an accomplished artist, with some paintings selling for hundreds of dollars. He loves animals, represented in many of his works. You can watch Mark describe some of his paintings at www.MarkRimland.com.

Like Dr. Rimland, parents of children with autism invest an enormous amount of effort and time in planning for the future. They wonder what their autistic child will be like in adulthood, and how much help will be available then. Will services be better than they are today? Or will they stay the same, or even get worse? What should families do to start preparing for the time when a child reaches puberty? What about adult living arrangements? Employment? Recreation? There is also the anxious question, "What will happen to my child when I am gone?" The parents of today's autistic adults have already dealt with these issues, and offer invaluable guidance to younger parents.

New "grown-up" thoughts and feelings are part of transition into adulthood. Many professionals and parents mistakenly assume that autistic teens don't experience typical emotional changes because some of them have a lower mental and/or social-emotional age. After talking with hundreds of teenagers and adults with autism, it's apparent that they go through this developmental stage just as their peers do, but in a less complicated manner. They're less likely to want to become independent of their parents, but just like all young adults, they're trying to figure out who they are and their role in society.

Emerging sexuality is one of the biggest issues for both parents and children, and behaviors such as masturbation in unacceptable situations and inappropriate sexual advances toward other people are a major concern. Physical changes create new challenges as well, such as the mechanics of shaving for boys.

Given the increase in the incidence of autism over the past 20 years, more and more parents will be confronting these issues in the very near future. The Autism Research Institute (ARI) is responding to this need by offering information and resources on sexual issues on a page on their website, www.autism.com. In addition, the Indiana Resource Center provides information on sexual issues at www.iidc.indiana.edu/irca. It is our hope that the book in your hand, combined with these resources, might show the way for parents facing an autistic child's journey into adulthood.

In closing, I would like to thank the many people who contributed to this project. Dr. Rimland would have been proud to see how well the book turned out. During the last year of his life he very much wanted to finish gathering and editing the material, but we were unable to complete the project during that difficult time. Some earthly angels appeared almost out of nowhere: Judith Chinitz, a parent of an autistic child and author of the book *We Band of Mothers*, was instrumental in contacting and gathering the final chapters for the book. Judy, thank you very much for your outstanding work. Two other angels, Anne Van Rensselaer and Jane Johnson, heard about the project and volunteered to edit the book. Within a relatively short period of time, the book was finished and a publisher was found. Anne and Jane, thank you for your hard work and dedication. You did a great job!

Above all, we owe a debt of gratitude to the families who have shared their wisdom with us, both in the pages of this book and throughout the years of ARI's existence. Their courage in contending with so many challenges and roadblocks is a testimonial to the strength, determination, and love within every one of us.

Stephen M. Edelson, Ph.D.
Director, Autism Research Institute
San Diego, California
June 2007

ONE

Helen Landalf

A handsome middle-aged man with graying temples strolls the sidewalks of Kensington, a newly upscale neighborhood of San Diego. He stops by the outdoor tables at Starbucks to greet friends, then heads to his favorite hangout, the Kensington Coffee Company, for an iced cappuccino. After a quick glance at one wall of the café (graced by some of his own wonderfully colorful paintings), he settles down at a window table to read the newspaper.

If you were to sit down with this man, you might at first think that he's just a regular guy enjoying his afternoon coffee. But if you stayed, you'd realize he doesn't quite understand the give and take of a real conversation. He talks a little too loudly about things, and too much about people you don't know. He tells you all about himself, but he doesn't seem that interested in you.

That's because he has autism.

Almost everyone in Kensington knows this man. They might know him as Mark Rimland, the late Dr. Bernard Rimland's son. They might know him as the partially recovered autistic man who was one of Dustin Hoffman's models for his role in the film *Rain Man*. Or perhaps they know him as the talented artist whose work has appeared in galleries and books, and even on CD covers.

To me, he's just Mark, my big brother.

When I was born, Mark was already two years old. Infant that I was, it was impossible for me to appreciate how challenging it was for my parents to deal with an autistic toddler and a newborn baby at the same time. I don't remember much about our early days, but some stories have become family legend: the way Mark would scream when our mother changed her dress; his fascination with the vacuum cleaner, and a complete lack of interest in people; the fact that one physician who examined him told my parents they should put my brother in an institution and forget they ever had him.

I was too young when these things happened to remember them, but as I got older, I became aware that Mark was somehow different. Several mornings a week, he threw screaming fits because he hadn't had time to dress his dolls, which had to be meticulously taken care of in a particular order each day. He had inappropriate fits of giggling at the dinner table and often had to be sent into another room. But even more fascinating to me was Mark's uncanny ability to remember the exact date and time that something happened. If you asked him, "When did we get our cat, Mark?" he'd answer, "At 10:35 on June 21st, 1961. It was a Thursday." And he might even add, "It was cloudy."

The birth of my younger brother, Paul, made Mark's deviations from normal even clearer to me. Although Paul was quite a few years younger than I was, we were able to interact and play with each other in a way Mark and I never could.

When I started school, I was aware that Mark was receiving an education too. I remember coming into the house one afternoon to see Mark working with a tutor who was teaching him to read by giving him M&Ms as a reward. With the self-interest of a seven-year-old, I was struck by the unfairness of the situation: I was learning to read at school; why weren't my teachers giving me M&Ms?

During our teenaged years, my awareness of Mark's differences increased. While I was involved with music, drama, and dance and had an active social life, my older brother spent much of his time when he wasn't in school sitting in a rocking chair, rocking back and forth while he listened to the same phonograph records over and over.

I was aware that other people noticed Mark's differences, too. On Friday nights, Mark liked to play pool at the neighborhood church Youth Hall. Apparently the other teenagers teased Mark, because he came home one night and asked me, "Am I retarded?" I didn't know what to say. I knew my brother was autistic, not retarded, but wasn't he really asking, "Am I normal?" There was no good response to that.

At sixteen, I got my driver's license. This was a real turning point for me, of course, but it was for Mark, as well. I remember him asking, "How come Helen is younger than me, and she can drive and I can't?" His question haunted me and injected a dash of guilt into my newfound freedom.

There were definitely times when I felt guilty for being able to live a normal life when my brother could not, through no fault of his own. I'm sure there were times I was jealous because Mark needed more of our parents' attention, and I probably felt guilty about that, too. But mostly I felt protective of my older brother who functioned more like a younger sibling, even though he was two years older.

Although Mark's childhood was difficult, in a way he was extremely lucky. He had the advantage of having a father who was at the forefront of autism research, so he was always the first beneficiary of my father's discoveries. I grew up watching him swallow a multitude of pills each day, little knowing that he was participating in my father's now-famous studies on the effect of mega-doses of vitamins on autistic children.

My father's scientific research was beyond me; what I did understand were his attempts to encourage Mark to look and act as normal as possible. Like many autistic children, Mark had an unusual posture and gait. My father encouraged him to stand up straight and, when introduced to someone, to offer a firm handshake. To this day, Mark has better posture than most people I know.

It was more difficult getting Mark to stop giggling at inappropriate times. Many family meals were interrupted by my father shouting, "Stop giggling!" It frightened me to hear Daddy yell at my brother like that, but I could see the results: Mark's giggling fits gradually lessened, and now they are nonexistent.

One of the behaviors that my father was not able to change was Mark's habit of speaking too loudly. Whether it's because Mark can't hear himself talk or because he gets so excited about what he's saying that he forgets to modulate his volume, it irritated my father to no end to hear Mark's voice booming from down the street. Even in the last months of his life, he was working with Mark to lower the volume of his voice.

My father's dedication to Mark was well known, but he's not the only one; my mother has always been willing to drive Mark to the school that's best for him, no matter how far away. Currently, she drives from San Diego to El Cajon in rush-hour traffic so that he can attend Saint Madeleine Sophie's, a wonderful center for developmentally disabled adults. She also keeps him involved in extracurricular activities, including swim practice and Special Olympics.

Special Olympics has been an important part of Mark's life since he was 15. He competes in sports including floor hockey, swimming, skiing, and volleyball. In addition to the fun and physical conditioning these sports provide (and the many blue ribbons Mark has brought home over the years!), Special Olympics has broadened his world by giving him an opportunity to make friends with other athletes and with coaches, and he's also gained a degree of independence through going on overnight trips to compete in other cities.

But perhaps the most important thing our mother does is nurture Mark's artistic talent. His aptitude for visual art wasn't discovered until he was 21, when his teacher asked him to draw an eagle at school. Although Mark had never drawn anything (in fact had never even produced a scribble) he amazed his teacher with a wonderful picture of an eagle.

After that, he began doing artwork at school on a regular basis and also began taking private art lessons. As he learned to work in different media, including watercolor, acrylics, and computer-generated art, his natural ability developed by leaps and bounds. At first he was most interested in painting animals and landscapes, but now his paintings often feature people—a fact that may be indicative of his blossoming social skills and his widening awareness of others.

Mark's paintings, with their vivid colors and unique, sometimes quirky take on their subjects, have brought him a great deal of attention and praise. He's shown his work in galleries across the country, and his paintings have been featured on posters, greeting cards, and, most recently, the cover of a CD called *Daydreaming at Night* by musician Gregory Page, who Mark met on one of his daily rounds of Kensington. Several television stations have done documentaries on Mark's art, and he now regularly displays his work at Sophie's, a gallery connected to St. Madeleine Sophie's Center that features art by developmentally disabled adults.

By 1997 I'd published several books, and when I decided to write a children's book, I knew that I wanted Mark to be my illustrator. We both love cats, and after seeing one of his paintings titled *Kitten in a Basket*, I wrote *The Secret Night World of Cats*. With his art teacher Kathy Blavatt's help,

Mark painstakingly created illustrations to go along with my text, using both traditional painting and computer-generated art.

Mark had no trouble painting the cats in my story. His illustrations feature cats so vivid and lifelike they practically leap from the page, but painting the main character, a little girl named Amanda, proved to be problematic. His illustrations of her are flat and almost cartoon-like. At first, my publishers were unhappy about the discrepancy between the way that Amanda and the cats were depicted. But when I explained to them that this probably represented how Mark sees the world as a person with autism—animals and inanimate objects in the foreground, people in the background—they agreed that this actually added to the interest of the book, and they published his illustrations as he created them.

The Secret Night World of Cats was published in 1998. CBS This Morning did a spot about our collaboration. We did a number of signings at bookstores; all my life I'd wanted to create something with my older brother, and I was filled with pride as we stood side-by-side, pens in hand, signing the book we'd created together. The Secret Night World of Cats received a National Parent Publishing Association Honor Award in 1998, and is still in print after almost ten years.

Although we have yet to do another book together, Mark and I continue to have a close relationship, even though we live in different states. We have occasional phone conversations in which Mark updates me on his most current art project. He looks forward to my visits to San Diego, telling everyone he comes in contact with that his sister Helen is coming. In classic autistic fashion, though, no matter how excited he is to see me, he declines to vary his routine while I'm visiting. If I want to spend time with Mark, I accompany him on his daily rounds of Kensington.

Every time I see Mark now, I'm amazed by how much he's changed. He's gone from the child who wouldn't look you in the eye and was unable to speak in a full sentence, to a gregarious adult who knows how to make and keep friends and can even appreciate a good joke, a skill that isn't possible for most people with autism. He's gone from the boy who struggled to learn his letters in order to earn a handful of M&Ms, to a man who enjoys reading. He reads his favorite books over and over again, and is taking a class to improve his reading comprehension.

Along with Mark's improved social and cognitive abilities has come a decrease in his special, or "savant," calendar abilities. A number of years ago, if you told Mark the date and year of your birthday, he could tell you which day of the week you were born. I used to have him demonstrate this ability for my friends as a kind of parlor trick. Once, when I asked him how he did it, he replied by reciting a long, complicated mathematical formula that I couldn't begin to understand—a formula that he'd figured out on his own.

If you ask Mark to do the same trick today, he can still produce the correct answer, but it takes him longer than it used to. I like to think this is because, as he becomes more normal, he can no longer work on the problem with the intense focus so characteristic of people with autism. He's having a more difficult time shutting the world out, and that's a good thing.

As Mark leaves his calendar-calculation abilities behind, I see him taking more pride in himself as a human being. He sees himself—as he should—as an artist, an athlete, and a man who knows how to make friends. He's beginning to identify less with people with developmental disabilities, and more with normal folks.

One of the most striking changes in Mark is his new ability to tolerate change. People with autism cling to routine, and through much of his life Mark has been no different. He had routines for dressing, for eating—he even had to water the lawn in a certain way. But recently there have been monumental changes in Mark's life, and he's coping surprisingly well.

When we knew that my father was dying, a major concern was how Mark would cope. During my father's illness, my mother was careful to keep Mark's daily life as normal as possible. He went to school, to Special Olympics and art lessons, and he did his daily round of the Kensington coffee shops. We weren't sure what grasp Mark had of the concept of death, and we were worried he might become unhinged by such a huge change in the family.

When I came home for my father's funeral, I was still unsure how Mark was dealing with the situation. But when I walked into the room, he looked at me calmly and said, "Did you hear that Daddy passed away?" There was no huge display of emotion, but looking into my brother's eyes, I could tell that he had grasped the finality of our father's death. Although his capacity for the expression of feelings differs from mine, I have to believe that, in his own way, he feels the same deep sense of loss that I do.

Although I've seen huge improvements in Mark over the years, many challenges still remain. He is comfortable in the places he knows—his neighborhood, his school—but he has little experience of independent living in the larger world. On the rare occasions that he travels, my mother packs Mark's suitcase, labeling each article of clothing with the day of the week he is to wear it. She alerts the airline personnel, who assist Mark on the plane, and he must have someone meet him at his destination. He has only a rudimentary understanding of money—he knows how much a cappuccino costs—and he depends on my mother to feed him, transport him, and keep track of his weekly schedule.

Yet, in spite of the challenges, Mark has a good life. He is comfortable in himself and enjoys everything he does. That's more than I can say about a lot of "normal" people I know.

People sometimes ask me what it was like to grow up with a brother with autism. "That must have been tough," they say. "Weren't you jealous of how much attention he got?"

Some things about growing up with Mark were tough, but, in retrospect, I feel my experience of having a sibling with autism has made me a stronger person. Through Mark, I learned compassion at a young age. I was never tempted to join in the usual schoolyard occupation of relentlessly teasing anyone different.

I believe that growing up with Mark has given me the capacity to see beyond a person's disability, and to appreciate him or her for who they are. In fact, I'm now happily married to a man who has cognitive disabilities due to the removal of a brain tumor. His level of disability is nowhere near Mark's, of course, but I know that having an autistic brother enabled me to see beyond Steven's cognitive challenges, and to embrace the wonderful human being that he is.

Most important, I think having Mark as a brother has taught me never to give up on someone. Just as the boy who doctors told my parents was hopeless and belonged in an institution is now a happy, well-adjusted adult, I believe that given enough love, attention, and advantages, anyone can overcome the challenges life hands them. In my roles as teacher and stepparent to two teenaged boys, I am given opportunities to put this belief into practice every day.

No one is sure what Mark's future holds. Will he continue to improve, so that one day he can live in the community as a fully independent adult? Or is he now functioning at the highest level possible for him? And what will happen when my mother can no longer care for him? Will my brother Paul and I become his caretakers, or will he live in a group home with other developmentally disabled adults?

I push these questions away when they begin to plague me. I will deal with them when the time comes. For now, I celebrate my brother the artist, the Special Olympics athlete, the caring human being and am grateful for how far he has come.

TWO

Joan H. Goble, MD

We were fortunate to read Dr. Rimland's book back in the early 1960s, when we needed it most. Our son John Robert suffers from classic infantile autism. Now almost 43 years old, he has a job and an apartment of his own in a HUD building supervised by nuns. He also has a driver's license, and can shop, cook, clean house, and use the local transportation system.

My husband and I have had many autistic and handicapped patients in our pediatric ophthalmology practice in San Mateo, California, and over the years I've had occasion to talk to many of their parents. I've learned three "pearls" that I tell anyone who has to deal with a handicapped child.

The first is this: *each day is a new day*. If we've made a mistake in dealing with our child, it's not fatal (regardless of how the psychotherapists make you feel!). If we've set too high a goal that day, or lost our temper and yelled, we must remember that this just gives us information we'll need to deal with problems tomorrow. And if we can't manage that day, there's another tomorrow. We must not carry guilt forward—very important.

The next pearl is: *you count, too*. We must give ourselves a chance to live our lives and be there for our other children. Sacrificing ourselves for our handicapped child teaches them that they're the only people who deserve consideration, a very bad message. They must eventually be able to live in this world, and must learn that other people are entitled to consideration. We parents need respite, and consideration too.

The last pearl is this: *even if your child does everything he can to convince you he doesn't want limits, you must not give in; you must set them.* You can demonstrate the importance of this to yourself by the experiment of *not* setting limits, and watch him fly apart.

We've watched with pleasure as John has developed into a man with a life and a future. I hope this note is of use to someone.

THREE

Jean and Michael Curtin

My son Michael looked like a very thoughtful baby. He seemed overly preoccupied, and intelligent. He was also hyperactive; he rocked on all fours in his crib all night long, starting at four months of age. He was the only baby I have ever seen who grabbed the bars on a baby swing, stopped it, and tried to climb out.

Not only did he seem to be allergic to everything on the planet, but heat, cold, motion, and change evoked exaggerated responses as well. By contrast, Michael seemed impervious to pain, indifferent to hugs, and lost inside his own head. He showed no interest in Christmas presents, age-appropriate toys, or playmates. Although he accomplished a number of rather amazing feats (he assembled his sister's doll stroller, right down to the washers, with no instruction, at age three), Mike was thought of as "slow." His blank face made him appear to absorb little, if any, of the outside world.

Some thought him deaf or even blind, although testing was "normal." People would approach me to offer advice. Some suggested that Michael was "demon-possessed," others, that he was "retarded." Still others thought that my son was a genius with a sensitive temperament and that he would grow up to be a rocket scientist. Over time, the most accurate word to describe Michael was *changeable*. One moment he would be laughing hysterically, and the next he would be screaming or withdrawn. This could last for ten minutes, or all day long. If the wrong thing happened (i.e. someone spoke to him or touched him when he wasn't expecting it), he was a wreck for the rest of the day. He would slip behind his wall and not come out—or worse, he'd hit, scream, kick, punch, pinch, or bite.

Moreover, his spinning in circles, lining things up in doorways, sleeping for only a few hours a night, and difficulty with transitioning, from changing clothes to going outside on a rainy day, were overwhelming for us as parents. In time, we realized that Michael was communicating with us that these things were equally overwhelming to him. Worse, from his viewpoint, his life was a series of unpredictable, random encounters with beings who screamed in his ears, pinched his skin, came into and out of his field of vision without warning, took him places he'd never go if he had a choice, and caused him to have headaches all day long.

> I used to hit my head on the wall. This was a way to block out the rest of the world's painful, relentless madness. It was a way to connect to it also. I still felt enough to not completely space out and cope slightly with the world around me by blocking out the pain. It actually felt good, one of many things I used when the world was too overwhelming to stand. (Michael Curtin, *A Real Live Boy*, publication pending)

What's really going on in kids like Mike is the lack of ability to modulate sensory input. The filters that are built into the nervous system for sorting out incoming information are damaged. This is exacerbated by a feedback loop that over-stimulates the parasympathetic nervous system, causing a continuous "fight or flight" reaction in some kids. If you've ever been scared out of your wits, you know that it's unpleasant and that it's difficult to calm down afterward. Now imagine this happening every day, all day. In some cases, this hypersensitivity extends to the digestive system, causing pain and anxiety. And if your child has an inability to pay attention or store information, as Michael did, the world is even more confusing.

I compare this to being stuck on 33 rpm speed, and having the rest of the world moving at 45 rpm. Everything seems to be coming in too loud, too fast, too much. This overload causes defensive withdrawal: you find a spot where the world's not moving so fast, and you defend it. You find one thing that you can make sense of in some way, and you do it. The only sensory input you can stand is your own. Everything else you block out if you can, because it makes no sense. Worse, it hurts.

Because you're spending all of your energy protecting yourself from pain, or coping with it, there's no time to learn from the environment and no way to safely explore it. Since exploration is how children learn, there's no pain-free way to learn for these children! To add to the confusion, it appears to other people that nothing is getting through to the child, so they exaggerate things way too much.

How did I learn to help my son? And what did he teach me that can help you to help your child?

The first toe in the door to Michael's world came when an allergist had us remove all food dyes, preservatives, corn, wheat, and milk products from his diet. This brought dramatic changes in his behavior; he calmed down, started pointing and gesturing, and began using words. I believe that the exaggerated sensitivity seen in the nervous system of many of these children is symptomatic of a matching exaggerated immune response. In these cases, balancing the immune system can establish balance in the nervous system. For this reason, a trial of vitamin B6 and magnesium together, per Dr. Bernard Rimland's guidelines, is worth a try in kids like Michael. Addressing heavy-metal poisoning, fungal infection, viral activation, and irritation throughout the GI tract can remove some of the "white noise" in the nervous system.

In Michael's case, his "observable IQ" jumped from 50 to 70 with dietary changes, enzymes, B6, and anti-fungals. It did *not* cure his autism or fix everything. It *did* help him cope with the world a lot better. DMAE, a compound related to B-complex vitamins, helped him to focus on things outside his head. It helped him get his words out, and express himself in more appropriate ways. More importantly, it sparked an interest in imaginary play—something we'd not seen before.

It is critical to understand that these are internally focused kids and that, by means of vitamins, ABA, medications, etc., it's possible to capture their interest and to build an externally focused, purposeful attention span. Without that essential shift, progress will be greatly limited. Eliminating the hyper-arousal of sensory input to a damaged nervous system is the starting point for enabling these kids to develop interest in the world around them.

Michael had a formal developmental evaluation when he was three and a half. The improvements we'd seen in his behavior were reflected in the lead physician's observation that Mike was "friendly" and proud of his own accomplishments. Nonetheless, his rigidity, perseveration on cars, inconsistent processing ability, lack of attention span, and sensory issues were also prominent throughout the report. As I read the notes from the speech therapist and the psychologist, I was curious about something that seemed to be at the heart of the problem. In many situations, Michael appeared to be actively avoiding people. As I looked through his baby pictures, gaze aversion and evasion of the person holding him were visible going back to three months of age. Photographs and videos of infancy and early childhood may help you sort out what's happened with your child as well. At age 42 months, most of the interactions Michael had with people were forced, even with all of the progress he had made. Left to his own devices, he still didn't voluntarily approach people.

I did a log of his activities for a few days, just to see what Mike would do on his own. (This is another tool I highly recommend.) Throughout my observation period, he spent most of his time lining cars up in doorways, spinning himself in circles, and engaging in other activities that to an outside observer would seem purposeless. In fact, he was spending all of his energy blocking out painful stimuli and trying to perform his own version of sensory integration. All babies explore their environment through their senses. How do you explore the environment when doing so causes pain? When things are disconnected?

> I started spinning myself in circles, for hours on end. It was a new way of coping that helped me block out painful noises and feel myself exist. Eventually, after a long time of handling this, and then only after hours of doing so, I could think, over the noise and pain I had blocked out, which I couldn't before. Then, from there, I started being able to see, my eyes could focus on the larger world while spinning, slowly, that blur turned into tiny amounts of not completely seeable, but distinguishably they were objects. (Michael Curtin, *A Real Live Boy*)

As heart-wrenching and scary as the developmental evaluation was, having the observations of trained professionals to use as an objective yardstick to measure "normal" behavior against Michael's was a turning point. I could see the overwhelming job ahead of us, but I could also see, with tremendous gratitude and relief, the enormous hurdles we had already overcome. I read a number of very helpful books, including *Solving the Puzzle of Your Hard-to-Raise Child*, by William Crook, MD, and *What to Do About Your Brain-Injured Child*, by Glen Doman. The most enlightening book of all was *The Ultimate Stranger*, by Carl Delaccato. Chapter 8, "On reading the sensory problems," was especially illuminating. (I highly recommend those books, along with *Children With Starving Brains*, by Jacqueline McCandless, MD to anyone attempting to unlock their child's potential.)

I learned two valuable things from the experience: first, that Michael's avoidance of people wasn't personal; its purpose was to avoid pain. If he were ever to have more interaction with people, we were going to have to find a way to interact with him on his terms. Second, he was to me the bravest little boy on the planet. Every interaction he had with people hurt, yet he was determined to reach out to us, in his own way. He needed love, he deserved respect, and he was scared. As baffling as his behavior was to us, we were equally baffling to him. Somehow, that had to change.

After reading Dr. Crook, Doman, and the others, I started experimenting to find some kind of sensory input that wasn't painful to him. First, I discovered that squeezing Michael's hands made him relax. This was the cornerstone for developing a sensory therapy program. My next experiment was to test the theory that Michael was pretty much living inside a sensory prison. For one whole day, I sat on the floor next to him and did not move. I did not speak to, look at, approach, or even think at my son. All one day and late into the afternoon the next day, he drove his tiny car up and down the ramp to his Fisher Price garage, seemingly oblivious to my presence. Then unexpectedly, he turned around and smiled. Shyly he handed me a car and asked, "Wanna play?" I was too scared to breathe. I had just been handed the keys to Michael's private world. I gradually developed two complementary therapy programs, one for "odd" hours that was extremely structured, and one for "even" hours that included interaction with other kids. The purpose of the first program was to integrate Michael's senses. The purpose of the second was to get him to voluntarily engage in spontaneous interaction with other kids.

Michael wasn't forced to join in the activities, which were designed to be structured enough to not frighten him, but fun enough for all of the kids to enjoy. The concept of developing a child-focused, sensory-based approach is critical for some kids, especially those with sensory defensiveness. Enjoyable contact with others is the key to developing social interaction for them. As the environment becomes more tolerable and people become more predictable, the sensory overload is reduced, and natural curiosity and the desire to explore the world and interact with people gains strength with practice.

It's important to help these young children develop self-care skills, no matter how small. I bought identical sets of pull-on pants and shirts with soft insides, and socks that were easy to pull on. I bought a small pitcher and over-sized drinking glasses that were hard to knock over. Michael got to put his clothes on and help pour his own juice. He was very pleased at being able to do things for himself. It helped to offset his general passivity about acting on his environment, in a functional way.

Using the things Michael loved most (cars, deep touch, a head and neck massager, a little bus that he loved to turn on and hold in his hand), I was able to reward Michael for persisting through things that were hard for him. I was careful to save food rewards (limited to "safe" treats) for the most difficult tasks. I bought a brightly colored puzzle mat with a town on it, including a road with a yellow center line (one of his perseverations). At first, my sitting near while he drove his car across a tiny corner of that mat was too much for him. Gradually, he was able to tolerate my presence, and he would put up with my commentary on what was going on. Eventually, he handed me a car to drive on the mat. It was a long time before my car could join his in driving all over the mat, and even longer before I could use my fingers to "walk" from the car into the library, store, etc. The key to eventual success was sensing when to "push" and when to back off.

I capitalized on his distractibility and love of small cars by keeping little cars in my pockets to stop him when he was about to melt down and hit another child. Meltdowns were usually precipitated by someone touching one of his carefully placed piles of cars, moving too quickly, or intruding on his space. I also used these cars to discipline Michael when he hit someone. I would speak directly into his ear, holding him so that he was facing away from me. I would say emphatically but calmly, "No hitting," and put his toy of choice on top of the refrigerator. These toy-car "time-outs" were only two minutes long, but they were effective. Between the supplements Mike was given and the consistent system of rewards and punishment, he was slowly beginning to grasp the principle of cause and effect, albeit in a limited way.

Michael slowly became more tolerant of new surroundings, different people interacting with him, and changing situations. We gave him foam earplugs to wear whenever we were visiting friends or family, or going to a support group meeting. This made a tremendous difference for him. Our family method was expanded to every person who came into contact with Michael, and it was expected that they'd use the same tools that we used to shape his behavior. We also worked hard to ensure that the expectations of everyone who interacted with him were consistent, and that he didn't "get away with things" (because he could pick up on people's expectations of him in a heartbeat!). The programs I was working on were passed along to friends, relatives, neighbors, and sitters, and turned into simple games that were fun not only for him, but also for other kids. In this way, we could be certain that Mike could process certain information in many environments, and with different people.

Using simple tests and books on child development, I went through Michael's senses one by one, scanning for development gaps. Using milestones for normal development from a number of sources, we slowly pieced together the areas where he still had delays, then came up with activities that addressed these issues. *Without the supplements, dietary intervention, and the intensive effort to break down the sensory defensiveness, any attempt to close the developmental gaps would most likely have been fruitless.* It's important to understand that the "stims" he had were purposeful and functional from his point of view. Our approach to limiting these stims was to find ways to do for Michael the things he was doing to himself. In this way, he could get the sensory input he needed without "tuning out" the rest of the world. When he absolutely had to withdraw for a bit, he could request a time-out; he'd get into a playpen and drive one of his cars back and forth until he was ready to re-emerge. Whenever this happened, our response to his request was *completely neutral, without any inference that this was a "good" or "bad" activity.* These time-outs helped him process the changes he was going through, and prevented many meltdowns.

Michael was five years old before he could finally begin to learn naturally, starting with Auditory Integration Therapy when he was five and a half. It allowed him to be free of the excruciating "bees" and "motorcycles" in his head. Vision therapy followed a year later. Finally, at age seven, he could both "see" and "hear." Although he entered kindergarten without an educational classification, he was in sixth grade before he really came into his own, able to make friends, talk about school after he came home on the bus, and be spontaneous. Today, at 20, he's an articulate, intelligent, likeable young man, with a deep sense of compassion for parents of children with autism. He has goals; helping parents understand kids like him is one, and helping people use the right foods, lifestyle changes, and supplements to stay healthy in a polluted world is another.

Mike and I are working on a book together. We can be reached for speaking engagements at j_m_curtin@yahoo.com.

FOUR

Katie Dolan

Advice for young families

- In the beginning, there is family.

- Nothing is more important to the survival of the child with autism than a strong family, an extended circle of support from relatives and friends.

- Father and mother MUST have at least one weekend a month to re-create themselves, together, alone, going out with friends, following their bliss/hobbies, etc.

- Get grief counseling—it's important to say goodbye to the child who never was and never will be, and to become acquainted with your real child with autism.

- Don't fall in love with autism—sometimes as parents we get caught up in the mystery and even the magic of autism, so it's important to recognize it's not something to be revered, but a condition that requires realistic parenting if the child is to survive.

- *Teacher* is the most beautiful word in the English language.

- Find parents of older kids with autism who can mentor you, and parents who are in the same boat as you, who can partner with you in mutually helpful ways.

- Get on the internet; learn to write well; use e-mail for networking of information and support.

- Above all, find the latest, most appropriate techniques for teaching your son or daughter with autism to communicate early. And never stop communicating with them.

- In the end, there is family.

FIVE

John Henley

When Sean was little, my dear friend Carol Croke told me that things would get better. She was one of the founders of the Autism Society of Oregon, and I'm not sure if she said this because she knew I'd get past the grief of my son being autistic, or that she somehow knew that Sean would slow down, or perhaps she thought I might just get used to life with an autistic young man. When she told me this, her son Tim was nearly the age Sean is now; just as it did for her, it has gotten better for me.

The fear of what's to become of Sean after I die haunts me, like some recurring monster in a series of movies that never ends. Intellectually, I know we're supposed to keep the future where it belongs. I know we aren't supposed to have expectations, only plans. I know all these things, but what's in my heart is stronger. It's good, as a parent, to have a variety of support groups; spend time with people who share difficulties, or a community that has some spiritual program in common with you. If nothing else, these support systems alleviate my fears. Just as your child never has enough services, you can never have enough of your own supports.

Sean doesn't have any siblings. After his diagnosis a number of family members, and friends too, seemed to step back and out of our life; the chances of his extended family giving him lifestyle support are slim. Even if he had siblings or wider family support, I don't think it would be fair to ask any of them to give up their plans for his sake. There are no group homes that we trust available to us at this time, but perhaps this will change. We're fortunate enough to own our home, and should be able to arrange a living trust for him so he can stay there and have around-the-clock caregivers to keep an eye on him. He has epilepsy, which doubles the need for someone to watch over him.

When Sean was little, his autistic behaviors intrigued people. When he got older, his "stimming" and other behaviors alarmed them. Thanks to nutritional intervention, his autistic behaviors are relatively light and not continual, but I can't say they're totally under control. He can attend movies and go out to a restaurant, and for the most part not draw too much attention. If you're not familiar with Dr. Bernard Rimland's work with vitamins and nutritional intervention, I strongly recommend you find out about the program. It's thanks to this protocol that Sean is doing as well as he is; it's the reason that he can focus on a task, and hold a part-time job as an adult.

When Sean was in school, while he may not have been getting the interventions he needed from the school district, at the very least he had tasks to perform and a place to go, and that was preferable to his hanging around the house. Once he was out of the school system (age 21 in Oregon), we were very fortunate to find a county-run program that supports people with disabilities. A young man named Paul See has been Sean's job counselor and has done marvelously with him. Thanks to Paul, Sean got a job coach, and then a job with a local grocery store chain.

Dealing with county and state-run programs is both easier and harder than dealing with the educational districts. There are laws dictating how children with autism receive a public education, and when your child is young, you spend long hours going over Individualized Education Programs (IEPs) and talking with teachers and aids. When your child is an adult, you have more time on your hands because there are no more arguments or discussions with the school district. Battles with other parents about the use of aversive therapies, or whether Mesibov's or Lovaas's technique is more effective, no longer matter; in fact, what have you accomplished? You haven't done much to build your own support system, or a meaningful life for your child over the next 70 years (statistically speaking); the important question is: what is your child going to do with his or her day when you're not there?

The Americans with Disabilities Act declares that once a person with a disability is hired, the employer must enable that person to perform the job;

it doesn't say an employer must hire someone with a disability. If your child gets a job and a job coach, you don't have the legal leverage with the employer that you did with the school district. If the person with a disability becomes a danger to himself or others, or simply costs the employer too much money, the employer has the right to fire him. Proving that the employer has fired an autistic person on the grounds of prejudice is very difficult, akin to proving that an employer has fired or failed to promote someone on the grounds of sex, race, or religious persuasion. There are few, if any, advocacy systems to protect your child against abuses by employers. Perhaps labor unions will address this issue someday and such systems may come to be. But for now, you must cooperate with any employer willing to consider giving your child a job. You have to change gears. Employers are not teachers or school administrators. There must be a lot of give and take.

We are lucky Sean has a job that he likes, in a business that appreciates him. He sorts out the recyclable materials while the job coach makes sure that he doesn't get into a jam. Sean is capable of problem solving, but it sometimes takes him a long time, and like the rest of us, he can make a wrong choice. When he was 16, he accidentally set a dishrag on fire in our kitchen. He dropped it on the floor and ran away, starting a small fire. The choice he made was to save himself. This was obviously a good choice, but he could have stomped on the fire, as I did, to put it out (had I not walked in, who knows?). My point is that Sean needs a job coach to help him make the right choices. Most of the time, he knows exactly what to do.

The grocery store is not quite sure how to handle the job coach. He isn't exactly a store employee, but he's responsible for making sure one of their employees gets his job done. It worries the store manager that they have someone working on the premises who is in some sense an insurance liability, as well as a representative of the business, but who isn't an employee. It's challenging for them, and we're very fortunate they're willing to accept that challenge. Like I said: give and take.

Sean's workweek is only about twelve hours, Monday through Thursday. The money he makes provides for his own health insurance, and gives him a little extra besides, but creates a problem in that it complicates his Social Security income. Because he makes slightly more than the law allows him, a very small portion of his SSI is taken away, so a Social Security agent has to handwrite a personalized and detailed accounting of how much money Social Security isn't giving him. (I suspect that the amount of money involved is not as much as the amount of wages Social

Security is investing in that personalized report. In fact, the handwritten accounting is vaguely reminiscent of an IEP!)

Like most adults, Sean has a daily routine. Every morning he is rousted from sleep and given his seizure medications, which are more or less effective. He lounges about listening to the radio and then gets up, fixes his bowl of rice cereal, no milk, and packs his lunch. His diet is the reason for his success as an autistic adult, and it's strict; no milk or food products with casein, no eggs, no refined sugar, no corn syrup, no preservatives, no wheat (or gluten from any source). However, there are now lots of products available to people with strict dietary needs. There's ice cream without milk, margarine without casein, gluten-free breads and treats, and there's always rice.

Sean needs to be coached about what to wear because he seems oblivious to the weather. He goes to work or to the YMCA to exercise. At work, the rest of the crew greet him. The young French girl who works in the bakery adores Sean and comes out to hug him. The African-American butcher has Sean do a complicated handshake with him involving no less than seven or eight steps, which Sean does very happily. Other workers give him a "high five" or simply say "hello." There are many who are not comfortable around Sean, but by working around him perhaps they'll learn that autistic people are not so very different from "normal" people. And then there are people who just don't like anybody, no matter what.

Sean's job entails sorting out the contents of five to ten rolling carts filled with recycled bottles, cans, and plastic containers. He goes at it hard and steady, and with the perseverance only an autistic young man can have. Employers—if you want something rather boring and tedious done, hire people with autism! The stream of recycling is never-ending, and Sean will have work for as long as the grocery store will have him.

They are delighted to have him because he is a nice young man, and they like him. However, we did have one problem. One of Sean's job coaches seemed to think it was his job to tell the store management how to do its job. The manager told us that either the job coach or Sean had to go. We told the job coach he had to stop criticizing or leave. He left. Now we have two great job coaches, and all is well. The point is that with autism, you can't turn your back on things, even if they seem to be under control.

In the evenings, Sean comes home and helps me do some chores, like cutting the lawn or emptying the dishwasher. Sometimes he simply enjoys his music. He doesn't particularly enjoy television, but given what's on I can't blame him. He can play some minimally interactive computer games. Stories that have some interaction are the best, such as the Living Books series, but there aren't many of these on the market.

During the weekend Sean goes with us to do the family shopping. He enjoys being driven around and watching things go by, and is treated with kindness everywhere he goes. We try to get him to make choices about things we're buying for him. This is sometimes successful, but often he doesn't seem to have an opinion. Also on the weekends, we like to have him run laps at the park.

We've tried to give Sean a sense that he's a participant in a team effort. He helps the family when it works; he plays with the family when it plays. He knows that he has to work to be a part of the grocery store. One of the things we did when he was in high school was to get him on the cross-country team. He proved to be very popular among his classmates, who elected him the "Most Inspirational" member of the team for three years out of four. He never came in first in a race, but he always kept up with his team. Whatever team can be built for him now might be what takes care of him when we are gone.

SIX

Gerda McCarthy

My son was diagnosed with autism before two; I noticed that he was withdrawn and not interacting with me, observations that led me to discuss my concerns with doctors, resulting in his diagnosis. At that time little was known about genetics, and whenever I asked professionals whether autism was inherited the answer was always, "No." I had touched on a territory unknown at the time.

"Will my baby be healthy?" is a question on every pregnant woman's mind, but mine especially, as I was experiencing dysmenorrhea (pain) without blood loss during the first trimester. My general practitioner ordered bed rest. From time to time, I feared that something was not quite right with my child-to-be. I felt only very weak fetal activity; when I asked the obstetrician during the seventh month of pregnancy if it wasn't high time my baby gave me a good kick, he simply answered, "Oh, it's just having an afternoon nap."

It seemed that my son began to develop normally, e.g. responding to "Clap your hands," appropriately. Right around his first birthday he developed a rectal temperature of 39°C (102.2°F) that lasted well past his second birthday. The cause of this strange fever was never diagnosed; it was only by chance that I took his temperature, because my mother and I noticed that his hands were very warm. During this period he looked well and was active, but he began to lose contact with the world around him, including eye contact.

The pediatrician was much more concerned by the lack of interaction than the elevated temperature. (My son was more interested in the doctor's shoelaces and the bedroom window than in the doctor.) He ordered an EEG test, which showed changes. He advised me to watch how my son developed. Unsatisfied, I brought my son to another pediatrician, who diagnosed autism. He arranged for a bowel biopsy to see whether there was any brain damage—there were no scanning facilities in those days. This procedure was done when my son was two years old.

Language emerged gradually, bilingually, as far back as nine months, but soon after my son's third birthday it gradually ceased. I devised a speech therapy when he was seven years old and within six weeks some meaningful speech, especially nouns, emerged. By the age of ten years, he developed challenging behavior. He was expelled from various schools.

In 1998, when my son was 24 years old, I initiated a brain-scanning research project with four other people with autism that resulted in a medical breakthrough. It showed in all participants a lack of blood flow both globally and regionally, in the right lateral temporal and right, left, and mid-frontal lobes, compared to controls.

My son's results:

- The images showed a generalized decrease in the uptake/retention of the HMPAO (a tracer compound) throughout the brain, with more marked perfusion deficits to both frontal lobes, both temporal lobes (particularly the anterior left and the entire extension of the right) as well as significant asymmetry at the level of the basal ganglia, with much lower tracer deposition on the left side.

- A careful examination of the entire study shows that this generalized decrease in the tracer deposition throughout the brain, including the cerebella hemispheres, may be of some importance regarding his clinical problem. It is presumed that the cerebella perfusion is decreased, which makes the relative quantification relatively unhelpful.

- In conclusion, it is important to stress this generalized decrease in the tracer deposition in the brain and cerebellum with more severe abnormalities in the frontal lobes as well as temporal lobes.

Neuroleptic drugs given to my son for his behavior gave him seizures. My husband and I were never informed of this side effect, nor of the drugs given. I pursued the matter only to be told that my husband had been informed. An easy excuse, since my husband died and I cannot ask him!

My son is being cared for at a National Health Service Trust and is doing quite well. The challenging behavior is better now. He is on a very low dose of Tegretol—not for epilepsy, but for his behavior. I give him Omega-3 supplements, which may well give him some help. He will be 42 years old on May 6, 2007.

SEVEN

Toby Arenberg

Ilene was born in 1961. It's been a long journey, and we couldn't be prouder of all that she's accomplished and what a kind, funny, delightful person she is.

In 1981, when she was almost 20, she "graduated" from a special ed high school and moved from our home to a group apartment run by Jay Nolan Community Services, a program that we helped start in 1975. She moved one week before her next-younger sibling went away to college. (She also has another brother, who left for college a year later.)

The Jay Nolan program is funded by California's Regional Center System (which never has enough money, of course). It started with a Saturday program in 1976; Ilene was in the first group, of 15 children. My husband Stan and I have remained very active with the Los Angeles Autism Society (under its various names) and with Jay Nolan Community Services. Stan has been on their board for almost 30 years, and served as president for three.

The story of how Ilene got to this point in her life is full of both successes and failures. As a young teenager, she had a speech therapist who did two very important things: she helped Ilene clear up a slight lisp, and she convinced us all that someday she could and would move out of our home. Ilene is the oldest of three, and true to the natural progression of life, she moved out first. In the beginning, she lived in group situations, but transitioned into supported living when she was 30. She moved to her own apartment with support staff from Jay Nolan and "No roommates!"—her decision.

Ilene is a whiz at typing, and took to the computer easily. She had a series of part-time jobs, and one full time job in an office. Unfortunately, that company went out of business. Soon after, she started taking a medical transcription course at a junior college about twenty miles away. She received her medical transcription certificate, and the Jay Nolan supported employment staff set out to find her a job. She has a pretty impressive resumé, but no medical transcription service would give her a job without experience. So, at Jay Nolan they designated a staff person to concentrate on finding a job for Ilene, and they found one at University of California at Los Angeles (UCLA), a short bus ride from where she lives.

She's been working at the UCLA Foundation since 1995, doing data entry and other chores in the office. She loves her job and is loath to take a vacation most of the time. The people with whom she works have been wonderful for her. Her vocabulary of what I call "casual speech" has increased remarkably. When she was 40, we had a birthday party for her and invited her boss, who called me to ask if others in the office could come too!!! Of course they could!

Since moving into supported living, Ilene has had a circle of friends to help her. The circle meets monthly at her apartment. The attendees are Stan and me, her two brothers, a good friend, and her staff—about 15 people in all. Ilene sets the agenda, calls the meeting to order, and thanks everyone at the end. We discuss the various aspects of her life: work, school, social/community events, medical updates, house maintenance, banking, etc., and plan the next meeting.

About a year ago, Ilene began taking medication to lower cholesterol, and on rare occasions, she might take an aspirin. She wears glasses that help her depth perception. She belongs to a gym, and goes occasionally. She's participated in a few 5K walks, takes the bus around town, tries new restaurants, and recently attended the wedding of a staff person in Texas (two members of her staff went with her). Every month, she attends a dance with staff, and has even gone on a date or two (with staff). We have no doubt that Ilene has come this far because of the wonderful people at Jay Nolan Community Services, and because we've been closely involved in its history: 30 years of dedication to a cause that has enabled Ilene and so many others to flourish. Back in the 1970s, we had a dream, and we worked very hard all the years since to continue that dream.

We have high hopes for Ilene's future. She's attended Santa Monica City College for about ten years, and by taking two classes a year will someday earn an Associate of Arts degree. We're confident that her brothers will always be a big part of her life, and we're all looking forward to attending her graduation ceremony. Since Stan is an attorney, of course we have wills and trusts and a special needs trust for Ilene, as well as a durable power of attorney for medical needs. She's been attending our synagogue with us for many, many years, and although she didn't go to Hebrew School, has pretty much memorized the services. Of course, we always will be fearful about the times when she's out there on her own, but so far, we've been able to help her through any emergency.

My two bits of advice for parents of children with autism:

- One, dare to dream for your child's future. Remember that adults should want to work, and if they can move a finger, there's a place for them to do so.

- Two, dig in and commit to making it happen. I've known too many parents who suddenly wake up when their child becomes an adult, and then whine about the lack of options. They should read the writings of Lou Brown, John O'Brian, Ann Donnellen, Martha Leary, and Jeff Strully. We were very lucky to be part of a group of parents who were, and continue to be, active advocates, dreamers, and creators.

EIGHT

Raymond Gallup

E ric was born on January 17, 1985, normal except for a cleft palate and lip. He reached the regular developmental milestones until he received the measles-mumps-rubella (MMR) vaccine on April 28, 1986, and then he regressed into autism. He lost all of his developing speech until he could only say "ca" (for car). He became hyperactive and wouldn't listen to what we said, as if he were deaf. We had to keep the front door locked, since he would run outside and down the street, sometimes with no clothes on.

In 1993 we read an article in the *Autism Research Review International* newsletter that mentioned Dr. Vijendra Singh's research on myelin basic protein antibodies in the blood of children with autism. After Eric was tested by Dr. Singh and found to be positive for these antibodies, we read an article by Cindy Goldenberg about intravenous gamma globulin (IVIG). It seemed that her son Garrett, who'd had autism, became normal after being treated with IVIG for several months, by Dr. Sudhir Gupta in California. We contacted Dr. James Oleske, a famous immunologist at University of Medicine and Dentistry of New Jersey, who agreed to test Eric. He found an immune dysfunction and decided to give him 18 IVIG infusions, between February 1996 and May 1997. Eric's cognitive and dexterity skills improved, but not his speech. Other parents sought treatment for their children by Dr. Oleske, and I know of one family in Westchester, New

York who had the same success as Garrett Goldenberg; their child no longer has autism.

I would recommend that parents have their child's immune blood panel tests checked for indications of immune dysfunction. Also, that they have a good gastroenterologist check (with both colonoscopy and endoscopy) for colitis or esophageal problems. Dr. Arthur Krigsman, a noted gastro-enterologist in New York, found that Eric has painful colitis. Dr. Krigsman recommended various medications to help with this problem.

When Eric was a child, we had problems getting him the proper educa tion. He was in two schools before we found one that was appropriate. Your township Board of Education may not be helpful, so it's important to push them to work with you to find the appropriate education. If they don't, then it's time to contact the State Board of Education, local state govern-ment representatives like state senators/state assemblymen, and your own disability/education/civil rights lawyer, to put pressure on your Board of Education. Also, it's always important to talk with other families when choosing a school.

When Eric was younger we hired a lawyer to draw up a will establish-ing appropriate guardianship in the event of our deaths. Without a legal will, the state takes over and has the final say in your child's affairs. In order to get Social Security benefits (SSI), it's important not to have large amounts of money put in the child's name. When one parent is unemployed and you meet the minimum requirements for getting SSI, you can apply. When your child reaches 18 it's important to apply right away at the Social Security office for SSI benefits as well as Medicare/Medicaid benefits for him or her, because it will take four to six months before the benefits come through.

Medical insurance didn't cover Eric's IVIG treatment at first; they said it was experimental. Unfortunately, medical insurance doesn't cover medical treatments for people with autism. The home nurses who were giving the IVIG treatments for Eric said that it was for an auto-immune problem (true) rather than an autism problem, and then insurance covered the treatment. Keep this in mind when you're trying to get medical interventions for your child with autism.

Children with autism like to eat the same foods all the time, and they don't tend to eat many vegetables or nutritious foods. My wife made sure that Eric ate healthy food, even if it meant he didn't eat. It was very tough to do this, but it was the only way we could get him to eat what he should eat.

When Eric was younger, we went to a neurologist who prescribed Ritalin and Prozac, which was a mistake. We shouldn't have had him on these drugs because they didn't help him, and they're known to cause problems. Fortunately, he only took them for a short time. Since then, because Eric has been biting, head-butting, kicking, and scratching me and my wife Helen, we've tried medications including Risperdal, Effexor, Zyprexa, Lorazepam, Abilify, Trazodone, Paxil CR, and Gabitril. Many of these drugs became ineffective over time. At this point, the opportunity for less invasive treatment for him is limited. This is why it's important to work on children with vitamins and homeopathic treatments when they're younger, before they become out-of-control adults. I wish the Defeat Autism Now! Protocol had existed ten years ago, when we could have used it for Eric.

Eric's sister Julie is 15 years old. She helps Eric when she can, but it isn't easy for her. She's had to see a psychiatrist because of the problems at home caused by her brother. Julie entered the Academy of Visual and Performing Arts, majoring in dance and drama. She was a representative in the World Special Olympics in Dublin, Ireland in Gymnastics for the New Jersey team in June 2003. She qualified because she's participated in Special Olympics since she was five years old, when Eric was involved. (The last year or two Eric hasn't been involved because of his tantrums.) Julie is now an assistant coach for Special Olympics in New Jersey.

Eric gets vitamin B-12 shots twice a week, folic acid, vitamin C, Super NuThera, trace minerals, and cod-liver oil, because of the high mercury levels that were found in his hair sample. These supplements help his body excrete mercury.

We used to try to restrain Eric when he tantrummed, but it led to more rage that lasted longer. Since he's stronger than us (over six feet tall, and 213 pounds) we have to lock ourselves in our bedroom or bathroom to keep from being hurt. We had to replace two bedroom doors with stronger ones, since Eric splintered them by kicking them in. I've had to call the police and the emergency people to transport Eric to the local hospital. I tell the dispatcher that Eric is strong and that he has autism. This way the police know ahead of time what they're dealing with. In February 2003 Eric chased me outside the house and bit my left index finger so badly that it was broken. If the neighbors hadn't intervened, I believe I would have lost my finger because he bit down so hard. Now two police cars show up with four policemen because they want to make sure no one will be hurt.

It's always good to have someplace to escape to so that events like this don't happen.

For those that have problems with aggression or self-injury, Kennedy Krieger Institute of Baltimore, Maryland has a Neurobehavioral Unit with a three- to four-month program with inpatient beds for 16. They only deal with children/young adults up to the age of 21, so it's important to address the problem early. Eric is on the waiting list and will be admitted soon. I understand that their program is excellent for dealing with difficult cases of aggression with autism.

We've spoken with the New Jersey Department of Developmental Disabilities (NJ DDD) to see if we could find an appropriate group home for him. Unfortunately, they told us that we had to accept a residential placement in Pennsylvania, two and a half hours away from our house. The facility had rooms that were locked, but we noticed there was a door by the kitchen area leading out to a back yard with a three-foot-high wooden fence and an open gate. Eric could've easily walked out the door and run down to the main road. NJ DDD told us it was our only option.

It isn't easy living with an adult with autism who's aggressive. As parents, know that other parents and autism organizations can help you, especially ARI, the Autism Research Institute. Also, know that there will be times when the state organizations such as the schools, local Board of Education, and the state disability organizations (such as the NJ DDD) will not be supportive of what's best for your child. I've approached a local group home, and am also working with other parents to get a group home up and running for all our kids.

We have to be pro-active for our adult children with autism because society isn't looking out for their best interest—only parents can do that.

NINE

Julie Gallup

When you're growing up, there's at least one person that makes a drastic impact on your life. My brother Eric is the one that stands out for me. Between watching *Sesame Street* together, going to the park, and doing puzzles, my love for him has grown. We've had our disagreements, but he was always there for me when no one else was. Everything about him isn't so flawless, though: my brother has autism.

I didn't know something was wrong with him until we started going out in public. Some people would stare at him like he was an animal gone wild in the zoo when he'd make a noise or run off by himself. I wouldn't be telling the truth if I said I wasn't embarrassed, but it also made me so angry that some people had no tolerance for my brother whatsoever.

Often I felt like the big sister, even though he was older than me. It was difficult for him to do certain activities by himself. We helped my parents rake leaves, even though most of them would fly away when he tried to put them in the bag. We all took turns reading to him when he wasn't "reading" in his own way, flipping through his enormous collection of books, making sure he caught every page. However, when it came to stealing a piece of cake from on top of the refrigerator, he mastered that.

Eric started getting really aggressive a few years ago. As soon as we saw he was getting agitated, we'd run into another room and lock the door behind us. I couldn't get over the fact that I was actually afraid of my brother. I knew he was in pain and had no other way to show it. The police were at our house frequently. Eric was transferred from hospital to hospital, but no place was right for him. I know it broke my parents' hearts, and mine too, but it was nearly impossible to give him 24-hour care at home.

We found a residential school for Eric in Delaware. Every other weekend, we take him out for lunch and ice cream (he'd eat all day if you let him). I look out across the water of the park we always stop at. I think about how I used to pray that God would somehow make him normal. Now, I think taking away his autism would take away some of his spirit too. I don't want to lose that. Eric has given me so much: the patience to deal with others, the ability to love and accept people for the way they are. I wouldn't be who I am today if it wasn't for him. Deep down, I think he knows this. All I can hope for him is that he lives the best life he possibly can and doesn't let anyone stand in his way. Maybe someday he'll be able to come home.

TEN

Clara Claiborne Park

Our daughter was born in 1958, when few MDs or psychologists were aware of autism, and those who did have an inkling of it were radically, harmfully wrong. The best advice we received back then came from a psychiatrist—despite his area of expertise he never so much as hinted at a "psychogenic" explanation for the strange eight-year-old he saw before him. Jessy was a whiz with shapes and numbers, but only just beginning to acquire intelligible speech. She'd made some progress since she was diagnosed at three, but she was still a textbook example of Kanner's early infantile autism, with every characteristic he described in place. It would have been natural, then, for this psychiatrist to recommend psychoanalytic treatment for her, and for us as well.

He did not. Instead he gave us what we needed most—encouragement for our home-based early-intervention program, and authoritative professional support for our efforts to get a few hours of education for her (and a bit of respite for ourselves). Even with his help, we were only partially successful—there was no IDEA law (Individuals with Disabilities Education Act, 1975) back then. But I never forgot his comforting and realistic advice, "Don't look ahead, even six months. You can't predict how far she'll develop; don't try."

Unlike higher-functioning, articulate adults on the autism spectrum (some with university degrees) who suffer to the point of bitterness because they see a gap between the jobs they hold—or fail to hold—and the jobs they feel they're qualified for, Jessy isn't burdened by that awareness. Her job structures her day and her life, and it provides simple social interactions she can (mostly) handle. All autistic people need social-skills training, but those with invisible handicaps need it most of all. Because her issues are apparent, no one expects Jessy to act like other people; in contrast, life is a lot more complex for university graduates with Asperger's.

Jessy thinks anybody who's nice to her is a friend. Sexual vulnerability is an issue for a person who has no comprehension of social cues or judgment in social situations. Behaviors that seem natural to her might be misinterpreted as provocative, or acquaintances might take advantage of autistic naiveté. We thought explicit sex education, at school and at home, plus cautions against "stranger danger" would be enough. We should have remembered what we'd learned in the years when we were teaching her to set the table, make her bed, vacuum, and cook: *Be specific.* Envision all the steps in the process, and teach them one by one. We'd forgotten that abstract information isn't enough for a person with poor understanding of social processes.

We hadn't considered the range of possible sexual scenarios. Could we have done so? Not all of them, of course, but we could have done better. We thought it was enough that she wasn't interested, and that ours is a safe community. It hadn't occurred to us to teach her to not go to a man's room alone, or to say "No!" loudly if someone touched her in a private place of her body, or even to scream (when she'd worked so hard at controlling screaming!). She was lucky; nothing serious happened, probably because her unresponsiveness disconcerted the offender. We only found out by accident that something had happened, and we would never have found out at all if she'd been living elsewhere. It takes long experience to know how to question a verbally impaired autistic person.

There are all sorts of reasons autistic children—or adults—can't live with their parents. We've been lucky; Jessy wasn't self-injurious, and she was passive rather than aggressive. She never needed drugs; we tried a couple, and some of Dr. Rimland's nutritional recommendations, but we noticed no change, and now Jessy takes only the usual vitamins. Passivity was in fact the problem, and lack of motivation was the big story. (Our story is told in detail in my two books, *The Siege* and *Exiting Nirvana.*)

We were lucky to be healthy, with no elderly parents or other unwell family members to care for, living in a town where we were able to attract a series of wonderful young people to help us, whose enthusiasm and creativity could take over when ours ran out. Home is the natural place for what I believe is called "incidental teaching"—incidental to all the events of daily life: the rituals of bedtime, the preparation of meals, repetitive chores, the family dinners, when even an autistic child has to learn to adapt (Jessy has three siblings). In adulthood, home skills training can continue as in childhood; slowly, gradually, one skill building on another.

Jessy continues to grow in capability. She can cook for herself, go to work (she's never late), and keep the house going, even while we're away. The psychiatrist was right all those years ago. How could we have imagined, let alone predicted, that at 45 she'd be finishing her 24th year in her simple job, paying taxes (she *likes* to fill out her tax return), and achieving international recognition as a painter? Not "cured," still recognizably autistic, but nevertheless a working, contributing member of her community and family. No large miracles, but that's miracle enough.

ELEVEN

Carol Croke

A t 41, Tim is still nonverbal, but he's doing well considering all the crummy things that were done to him in his adolescence.

Back then, there were no public classrooms or special services provided for these kids. Tim had been kicked out of all the private schools for disabled children when we were finally accepted into a college research study. It was degrading to us as parents to have 19-year-old students assure us they had a better grasp of our child's needs and behaviors than we did; they didn't. But how this program made us feel was nothing compared to what it did to him.

"Talk to him very loud to get his attention!" they said. In other words, yell at him. In those early years, neither we nor the professionals understood that Tim went into overload from excess stimulation. We know now this is a guarantee to set him "off." In fact, talking loudly or speaking in an argumentative or authoritarian voice, even if it's only on TV, might upset him. Like most autistic people, he's highly sensitive to his surroundings.

"Spray vinegar-water at his face, break an ammonia capsule under his nose or shock him with the cattle prod." They insisted these things would keep Tim from biting and hitting himself. Their theory on the cattle prod was that if they started with low voltage, Tim would get used to it and they'd have to increase it anyway, so a high voltage was used from the beginning. I used it only one time on him, and he overturned a table trying to get away from me.

"Rage Reduction" was another therapy they tried. Four staff members were used, each holding his arm or leg. One person would poke him repeatedly with their finger until he was frantic. When he reached what they called his "peak of frustration" they would slowly bring him down. At least that was their goal. But we never saw any positive results from it. "Rage Production" would've been a better name.

We were told he was too old to hug and kiss even though he was only seven. I went along with that for a short time and then decided *that was a bunch of baloney!*

Tim was a runner when he was young. He would climb out his bedroom window, scale the fence, and away he'd go. The "professionals" gave us many suggestions for eliminating this behavior, none of which worked. I finally used the same approach as I used on his brother and sister. Hallelujah! The plain old wooden spoon worked wonders! It only took two or three times. and he never left the yard again.

In the classroom things were repeated over and over to him, but he didn't respond—at least not in the way intended. Now we realize he needs time to process what he hears before he can act—it's a delayed reaction.

Tim demonstrates his frustration, pain, and sensory overload by biting his hand and hitting his head. At one point we had his retinas checked because his head hitting became so severe. Auditory Training helped reduce this self-abusive behavior. Now when he's upset, we can usually figure out that it's because he has a headache (giving him two acetaminophen (Tylenol) gelcaps calms him down within a few minutes), or someone or something is bugging him; that's when talking quietly and gently massaging his back and head goes a long way in calming him. His Dad will get nose-to-nose or forehead-to-forehead and talk to him. Tim will usually make eye contact and end up laughing.

I've found it's important to allow him to have time to go through his little rituals. Even when we're in a hurry, giving him the few extra seconds to do his thing matters less than the frustration he might go through if I try to stop him or rush him. So I'm allowing him to be autistic—well, he *is* autistic!

Happily, years ago he gave up his more elaborate rituals, like taking twenty or so full cups of water and lining them up in a straight row on his bedroom floor, or stacking the toilet bowl full of knickknacks, my Bible, purse, pictures, etc. Then there was his insistence that he must drag every-one's mattress and bedding into his own room. We were amazed that this little kid could pull a full-size mattress into his room and get it partway onto his bed.

Now his rituals are mainly tapping his finger on certain objects in a pattern, or tapping his teeth on a bottle of shampoo or lotion. Tim rocks back and forth, leaning on his down-turned wrists, where he's developed huge calluses. The Borage Dry Skin Therapy by "ShiKai Products" from the Nutrition Center works very well on these, and on the calluses on his hands where he bites himself.

He doesn't have many survival skills, but he smiles a lot and appears to be at peace. We feel fortunate that he's enrolled in a day program and goes out into the community. For many years this is what we prayed and advocated very hard for. We went through a lot of rough years, but with God's help and the patience He's given us, we survived.

In so many ways, Tim has been a blessing in disguise. I tell people, "Everyone needs a 'Tim' in their life."

TWELVE

Matthew DeLuca

As soon as you *know* something is wrong with your child, involve a qualified and competent physician who can identify the handicap as fully and quickly as possible.

I experienced guilt over having produced an imperfect child after my son was born, and then again many years later when we discovered he was autistic as well as retarded. An outside MD (medical doctor) tested our son at age four, and the results indicated that he had autism (as distinguished from true retardation). As was the practice in those days, the written findings were sent to our family physician, but not copied to us. After he retired 27 years later, I requested our son's medical file, where I found the letter indicating the autism diagnosis. Our approach, had we known, would have been directed toward accepting and treating autism rather than focusing on the original diagnosis of retardation. Finding the right doctor at the outset can reduce the guilt that parents feel.

The best decision I ever made was to accept help from Dr. Bernard Rimland at the Autism Research Institute. My son had been physically and verbally aggressive for many years, but after giving him the supplemental inositol recommended by Dr. Rimland, his aggressive episodes have diminished almost completely, although his autistic perseverations continue.

The worst mistake I ever made was allowing psychiatrists to experiment on him with the use of mind-altering psychiatric drugs, one of which put him in the hospital. We'd hoped the drugs would reduce the physical and mental aggression he endured in early adulthood.

Peter is now 46 years of age, and has adjusted to a homecare facility and daytime activity center. He loves to eat—it's his passion. He has a structured daily routine that's necessary in order for him to feel comfortable in his world.

My advice is based on long-term experience in trying to help my son: seek experienced professional help from people who are qualified and willing to work with you and your autistic child by using biomedical supplements.

Psychoactive drugs are blocking agents. While they might temporarily control autistic behavior, they can also prevent the possibility of improving.

THIRTEEN

Jinny and Bill Kemmel

My husband and I are the parents of a 48-year-old autistic son. For the first two years Bill appeared to be a happy, healthy, normal child, but then his behavior changed; he no longer made eye contact; he didn't respond when spoken to or called (we thought he might have hearing problems); he slept very little, and spent nights jumping up and down on his bed, laughing. We attributed the changes in his behavior to the birth of our daughter, and to our move across the country to Los Angeles.

When Bill's behavior didn't improve we consulted our pediatrician, who referred us to a psychiatrist. The psychiatrist did not wish to see our son, but spent time talking with me instead. This psychiatrist didn't seem interested in treating him, and after three or four visits I grew discouraged and sought help elsewhere.

Next we took Bill to Kennedy Child Study Center in Santa Monica, and were told that he would have to be institutionalized. Bill was seen by a therapist who was recommended by a child psychiatrist. The therapist saw him weekly, observing him. As far as we could tell, such treatment didn't improve Bill's behavior; he spent his time with the therapist playing in the water at her sink, turning the lights on and off, and running around the room, laughing.

Then we read the article in *Life* magazine about Dr. Ivar Lovaas and his work with autistic children at the University of California at Los Angeles (UCLA). Dr. Bernard Rimland and his book *Infantile Autism* were mentioned in the article, so we read the book, and contacted Dr. Rimland about our son. He was the first professional who seemed to have considerable knowledge about autism.

Dr. Rimland introduced us to Dr. Lovaas, who invited us to take part in his operant conditioning training for autistic children at UCLA. We asked our son's psychiatrist about taking part in Dr. Lovaas' program. The psychiatrist responded that he would refuse to see our son again if he participated in such program. His comment was that using operant conditioning with an autistic child "would be like throwing dirt into a surgical wound." We were desperate for substantive help, so we decided to stop the psychotherapy, and entered Bill in the UCLA program. He was six years old. During the program (about three years), there were significant changes to Billy's behavior. It was surprising to see the results with only Frosted Flakes as a reward, and raising our voices as a punishment. Bill's echolalia disappeared; he finally began sleeping through the night; he learned to read, and responded when called. He was by no means a normal child, but at least we were able to get his attention; we knew he wasn't deaf!

When we first started the UCLA program, he was *wild*. He would run around the room, turning the lights off and on, laughing and jumping up and down. Over time his behavior improved substantially, and he was able to participate in special education programs in the public school system until he was 21 years old. He functions fairly well now, although he still needs to be in a protective environment. We feel Billy's training at UCLA with Dr. Lovaas was his turning point. We have always been grateful to Dr. Bernard Rimland for opening that door for us.

After graduating from school, Bill went to work at a sheltered workshop in Santa Monica run by the Exceptional Children's Foundation. We taught him to take the bus, and he's become very good at finding his way around the West Los Angeles area. Twenty-seven years later he's still employed at the workshop. From time to time he's been placed in jobs outside of the workshop, but always in a protective environment with a job coach present.

Bill lived at home until he was 27, when he had the opportunity to share an apartment with two other handicapped men. A group of parents formed an unincorporated association to get a tax identification number and rent three apartments in a building owned by one of the parents. Three men lived in one apartment, two lived in a second apartment, and a supervisor lived in the third.

The parents and the men who occupied the apartments had known one another for years, through various groups for the handicapped. The supervisor's duties were to monitor grocery shopping and evening meal preparation in return for payment of his or her rent. Our unincorporated association became a vendor for the Regional Center and therefore received payment equal to the monthly rent for the supervisor's apartment. The parents met monthly with the resident supervisor to review any problems. This was a great situation for 19 years. But by 2004 all of the parents were now in their seventies and eighties, and the building was sold. The new owner wanted to move into Bill's apartment, so it was necessary to find other housing for the men. This parent group had worked well for many years, but housing provided by an established organization such as the one described below would provide a longer-lasting solution.

We were able to find Bill a one-room apartment in a building owned by an organization called Home Ownership Made Easy (a misnomer, since the facilities are rentals) in West Los Angeles. The organization owns 39 apartment buildings with units they rent to the handicapped. HOME has some funding from HUD (Department of Housing and Urban Development), and the rent is based on the income of the occupant. We were nervous about Bill living by himself, but two of the other apartments in the building were occupied by people who had 24-hour caregivers, so we were comforted knowing there were competent adults on the premises.

This situation lasted for a year. Bill has a very low frustration threshold, and tends to yell and scream when something goes wrong. Unfortunately the one window in his little apartment was about twenty feet from a bedroom window in the apartment building next door. The occupants complained about Bill making noise, so he had to move. Presently he lives in a two-bedroom, two-bath house owned by HOME. His roommate is a man with cerebral palsy who is confined to a wheelchair. The roommate attends a program during the day and has a caregiver from the time he returns in the afternoon until he leaves the next morning. This seems to be a good situation for Bill, since there's someone in the house in case of emergency. HOME has informed us that they will no longer make housing available for him if he can't control outbursts that result in complaints from the neighbors. Bill has been living at this location for about six months, and it seems to be working.

We are very happy with HOME and the dedicated people who work with the clients. They have a long waiting list of developmentally disabled individuals who need housing, so we're fortunate our son can be there.

Bill has a counselor who comes once a week to help him with finances, and another aid who comes each weekday evening to supervise dinner preparation. The aid also helps him plan his weekly menu and takes him grocery shopping. Both the counselor and the aid are employees of Creative Support Systems, which is a vendor with the Regional Center. Bill has his own bank account. He writes his own checks, with supervision. His checks from Social Security and the workshop are deposited directly, and I have his bank account online, so I can check almost daily to see that he's not overspending. Bill is able to take the bus to the bank, and draws out enough money to cover his expenses for the week.

In 2002 my husband and I sold the home where we'd lived for 41 years, and moved to be near my three sisters. We wanted to move Bill, but he's adamant about not moving. It's difficult being so far away from him, and it involves many trips to Los Angeles, but because he's so familiar with where he is and is so well known by the people who work with the handicapped, we decided to let him stay in the West Los Angeles area.

Treatments, pro and con

- By far, Bill's most beneficial treatment was the operant conditioning program at UCLA.

- Bill had a vasectomy before age 18. Although he's antisocial, we felt this was necessary. It was a very difficult decision for us because it felt as though we were giving up, but we know that he's not capable of parenting.

- We tried B6 and Dimethylglycine for a couple of years, but it didn't seem to help.

- When confronted with threats of having to move Bill because of his outbursts, we tried Paxil to try to calm him down, but it made him gain weight.

- We also tried Geodon, but he became too passive.
- We would not recommend using drugs.

Practical life tips

- Getting registered at 18 for Social Security and/or SSI is important.

- Registering with the Regional Center is important. They can be very helpful.

- Learning to take public transportation, if possible, is very important.

- Activities through Special Olympics and the Department of Parks and Recreation have been Bill's social life. They provide ongoing activities during the week and on Saturdays. He seems to enjoy all sports. Westside Special Olympics also provides at least one trip a year.

Bill still has very little conversational speech. He asks questions when he wants information, but when someone asks him a question his most common reply is, "I have no idea." Even though he does know the answer, he just doesn't want to be bothered with trying to gather his thoughts and form them into sentences.

Our hope for Bill is that he will reach his full potential, whatever that may be. We really don't know what he's capable of. Sometimes he really surprises us, like going to Kaiser Medical Center to get a flu shot by himself when I was late picking him up. We try to let him be as independent as possible, but because he's vulnerable, sometimes it's hard to let go.

Looking ahead to Bill's future without us, we have a trust leaving one-third of our estate to each of our two daughters, and one-third to them jointly, with the understanding that this third will be used as needed for Bill during his lifetime. Our oldest daughter has agreed to be his advocate.

FOURTEEN

Elaine Woodruff

Kristina's life was a fusion of color and sound when she was little, developing as she grew up into expression in art and music. She was almost traumatically affected by sounds when she was a child, particularly sirens. When we lived in Washington during the Cold War a siren blared every Tuesday at 11:00 a.m., and at the first beep Kristina would throw herself frantically into the nearest person's lap, block her ears, and scream. The grinder on the garbage collection truck was another disturbing sound. We found that turning on her little phonograph as loud as possible helped. She still becomes excitable at unusual noises, but she's no longer afraid.

She was about four or five when she began rough sketches of anything to which she was attracted, usually inspired by music. "Little Drummer Boy," which she played on her phonograph, was the source of one sketch. Another was "Spanish Eyes," a very long-lashed, very dark drawing of a single eye on which she printed the words "Don't Cry Spanish Eyes"; we had to make sure it didn't get lost during our travels in Europe. Kris was obsessive about particular possessions at certain times; for example, she had to have them with her before she could go to sleep. She's still that way about certain things, but her obsessions fade faster.

Her love of music developed early. She would sidle backwards into her Dad's lap with a record clutched in her hands, anything from Tchaikovsky to Smetana, as her selection for the evening. (We always wondered how she found what she wanted since she couldn't read yet.) When she did learn to read, it wasn't in the usual way; while she crawled nearby to improve her gait her father would repeat a word printed on a card placed in front of her. It worked.

Her art and her music are as one to her. She sees color in the sounds she makes on her guitar and in the music she hears: "I think of the color blue when I hear Dvorak's Fifth Symphony," she writes. "Whenever I strike an E note or an E chord I think of the color green."

She loved to do "scribble art" when she was little, so we kept her supplied with pads of paper, sketch books, crayons and markers, and were really surprised at how much she could do by herself, and even more surprised when she won a blue ribbon for a skyscraper she drew at the School for Contemporary Education (Falls Church, VA), a school that included non-handicapped students. Later her talent was nurtured at St. Madeleine Sophie's Center by her devoted art teacher, Kathleen Blavatt, who introduced her to computer art and other fine-art skills. She came by her sense of perspective naturally, and uses it in many of her paintings.

Her love of music is intrinsic to her life. Her brother taught her how to strum on his guitar and she took off from there, playing music by ear that she heard on the stereo, classical records, live music she loved—anything. We started her on basic guitar lessons when she was 15, and she played by ear until her longtime teacher Paul Grinvalsky persuaded us she could learn to read music. And she did. It continues to amaze me when I hear what are to me intricate instructions about fingering, timing, and technique, but which she follows without problem.

Kristina plans both her art and her music in advance. She writes in her journal: "Sometime this evening I'm going to draw a picture of a mermaid. I'll draw a mermaid's body, then I will draw two fins and a tail. I will also draw scales all over her body. I will spray the body light green. I will make her hair a red-orange color, then her face and body a flesh tone. The water is going to be blue-green." Kristina's dreaming about her art and music often distracts her from more practical tasks.

Aside from art and music her interests are varied, and change frequently. At present they range from science fiction aliens to the black holes in deep space, which she's drawn on her computer.

Dr. Robyn Young diagnosed Kristina as a "prodigious savant" in 1993.

Her art has been shown at Grossmont College, Mind Institute (UCSD), National Autism Convention, MacWorld, Pop Go The Arts, Folk Art

Festival, Junior League Auction, Wired Different show, and numerous local art shows. At the moment, it's on display at Sophie's Gallery (El Cajon, CA).

FIFTEEN

Ann Laferty-Snowhook

My daughter Eileen is 50, the oldest of five children. She has autism and cerebral palsy, and developed epilepsy at 38. She's mobile, but very fragile. Her speech is difficult to understand by all who don't know her well. She's a tiny person, often mistaken for a child. She's lived with her family for most of her life, and does so still. She isn't mentally retarded; I don't think many people with autism are.

She laughed at verbal puns before her fifth birthday. She's incredibly sensitive to emotional nuances, especially around her family and close friends. She has a sly sense of humor all her own. She's developed the ability to socialize with friends at the YMCA where she swims, with the support group from our church, and with our neighbors. She now *loves* to go on trips with us and settles into unfamiliar hotel rooms with amazing ease. When she was young she didn't want to go out at all. It took 40 years for us to figure out how to make her comfortable away from home. She needs *repeated* advance notice. She needs to know, immediately upon arrival, where her space (bed) will be at the hotel. We take a favorite object from home and have her put it on her chosen bed at the hotel so she knows where today's "home" is. And she needs to be with people who love her. As long as we prepare her ahead of time, she's comfortable, secure, and happy when traveling with us.

Daily life

My first and foremost advice is *always assume competence* and normal intelligence (except for a few gaps). Just because a person doesn't speak, or seems not to pay attention to what's happening, it doesn't mean he doesn't understand. And don't forget that a person with autism has wants and needs just the same as the rest of us. They have a huge obstacle hindering their communication with the rest of the world, but it isn't hopeless. They can and do learn, albeit *very slowly*, through our patience, empathy, imagination, and love.

Daily life can be hell on wheels one minute and joyful the next. Communication is the key to getting to the joyous days. Find any means possible to open the channels of communication, whether sign language, oral language, pantomime, written notes, and certainly augmented communication devices for those who have no functional verbal skills. Most "autistic behaviors," in my experience, are simple frustration at not being understood by others.

One of the most difficult times in life is puberty, and for children with autism it seems to be doubly hard. Outrageous behaviors multiply; self-control goes out the window, and listening to parents and teachers becomes much more difficult. It's the period when most pre-adult, out-of-home placements occur. The message to the teen-aged child who's sent to live with others is very destructive to his sense of self-worth and self-esteem. Ideally, intensive in-home and in-school supports should already be in place as adolescence approaches.

The expectation of and dependence on predictable routines seem to be a large part of autism. If you must change routines, give plenty of warning, and repeat it often before the change is made. Talk about new or different experiences. Try to give verbal pictures of what is going to occur. Write the information down; too much information is better than not enough.

Much has been made of the "raging" that many children with autism experience. My anecdotal experience suggests that raging is really a precursor to epilepsy. In fact, it may be another form of seizure. During a rage there is no volition and no stopping mid-stream, also characteristics of a seizure. It is a not-well-publicized fact that 50 percent of people with autism develop a seizure disorder by the time they are 40.

Another of the so-called autism experts' fallacies is the theory of "mind blindness"; it's thought that children with autism can't register or interpret our emotional attitudes and responses, but I've found this to be totally untrue. The response or acknowledgement of the emotions of others might be delayed, it may be inappropriate or conveyed in an odd way, but it's clearly present.

After completing school

Finding meaningful employment and activities is one tough proposition. For our non-verbal offspring, the prejudice factor is strong, because lack of speech equates with lack of smarts in our culture. A good supportive employment agency can be of tremendous help, and don't discount further schooling, whether academic or vocational. Most of our children are undereducated (possibly not so true now as it was in the past).

If your child has a skill, such as numbers, drawing, or anything else, do everything you can to help develop that skill so it can be used in the "real" world. The more competent he becomes, the more likely he'll be able to earn enough to stay out of poverty as an adult. And when he does find gainful employment, please make sure that a percentage is put in a sound investment for lean times (10 percent is a good sum), which everyone should be doing anyway.

Residential options

Ideally, children should live with their parents. Eighty percent of children with autism are boys, who get physically stronger as they get older, so this isn't always a viable solution. Dads often leave emotionally, but more often physically. The divorce rate is about 80 percent for families with autism.

Placement in a specialized foster home or small congregate (small group) home may be necessary for the safety of the rest of the family. But a congregate home, where three or four "consumers" with autism live with staff who are responsible for their care and well-being, is not a very good living solution for young people with autism; our autistic kids don't like living with other people with disabilities, especially autism. The unpredictability and chaos leave them without solid anchors and home routines. "Home" no longer means security in such settings. Most families could and would keep their children with them, if they had sufficient support.

As adults, most of our children with autism will wish to live in apartments or homes, like their contemporaries. There are good agencies that provide supported living services, allowing consumers to control their living arrangements, with whatever staff is necessary to allow them to function at home and in the community.

Supported living is an individualized service that's much better suited to people with autism than are congregate facilities. The adult can live without having to cope with the erratic behaviors of others, and with control over his environment and his staff. It's a successful model that's ideal for our children. Most of the staff are just doing a job, so constant supervision of both the environment and the staff by a family member is required to ensure quality of lifestyle.

The future

With the tremendous increase in autism (one in 150 births, according to the latest information from the US Centers for Disease Control), society will be fundamentally changed by the large numbers of people with autism.

I think there will be more tolerance for children on the spectrum, and far better methods for teaching them how to achieve their greatest potential. Some basic accommodations, both physical and social, will be made for people with hypersensitive perceptions.

Trusts

When thinking of your child's future, keep the vagaries of public funding in mind: i.e. the Regional Center system and/or the Department of Developmental Services. For instance, the Lanterman Act [California] is under siege now and will be again. Find a lawyer who knows how to write an unbreakable trust. Be as careful as you can to keep family financial assets out of reach of the state. "Special needs" trusts are even now being probed by several Regional Centers that are trying to capture the assets in order to offset Regional Center costs. According to our lawyer, who has an autistic daughter, a family trust that excludes the individual with a disability may paradoxically be the best defensive option.

Siblings

As if parents of disabled children weren't already stretched thin enough, time and effort need to be devoted to their other children. Siblings are inundated with feelings and emotions that children in other families don't have to deal with, and professional counseling can be a great help. And most of all, remember to keep siblings informed, so they feel like they're part of the family, not outsiders looking in.

SIXTEEN

Jordan Snowhook

My first-born, autistic sister is one year older than I am. Consequently, I took over the role of oldest child, which meant I ended up taking care of and protecting her, as well as our younger siblings. Please encourage your acting "oldest" child to develop outside interests and to not be an extra parent. And don't focus your family's entire existence around your autistic child. Don't cheat the rest of your children of a (relatively) normal childhood. It only breeds resentment, and the other siblings often run away at the first opportunity, through early marriage, joining the armed forces, etc.

SEVENTEEN

Elizabeth Snowhook

One very important tool our parents gave us was how to tell the rest of the world what was wrong with Eileen. Children need to know what to say when people ask, "What's wrong with your sister?" They need a simple sentence or two, such as, "Her brain was damaged at birth, so it doesn't work right." If people want more information than that, they will ask, so make certain your children understand in more detail. Siblings also need to be taught how to endure stares from the ignorant and impolite members of society. When a person stared, we made it a game to stare back in a very obvious way to try to make him uncomfortable, then we would explain what was wrong with our sister. Most people are just curious and are uncomfortable asking for details. Don't be afraid to open the door; you never know who'll end up being part of the autistic person's support system. "Eyes everywhere" are a good thing, in this case.

The most important thing we must all remember is that the autistic person is incapable of being anyone other than who he is. He cannot act any other way. *His brain does not function properly*, and it never will. He will get better, but he will never be "normal" and he will never be able to completely control his abnormal behaviors, so *don't expect it*. Try to truly understand his abnormal behaviors and compulsions so you can help him learn ways to get around or past them. Accept this—be grateful for the progress that he will make throughout his lifetime, and everyone will be much happier.

EIGHTEEN

Kim Oakley

On March 17, 1989, I held a healthy newborn baby boy in my arms. I'm the oldest of four girls, so I was thrilled to have a son, and my daughter looked forward to spending time with her new brother. His dazzling green eyes, wavy brown hair, and luminous skin brought compliments from family and friends, but several months later his developmental delays evoked my fear. I didn't know what autism was at the time—I'd never heard of it. I didn't know savage, uncontrollable behavior was in our future. I didn't know my son's cherub face would someday be bruised and bloodied by his own small fists. I didn't know the educational system would let him smash himself senseless in the classroom. I didn't know the California state agencies that serve disabled people weren't equipped to help my little boy stop hitting himself. Nor did I know there were people who'd oppose treatment that stopped him from hitting himself. But I know better now; I know better because I've spent the last 13 years raising a severely autistic child with compulsive self-injurious behavior (SIB).

I open the memory bank of the madness of our family's life to see what lingers. There are glimpses of joy and pieces of tattered lives on file. I'm there, but I'm living in a constant state of shock. I can hear my son sobbing. The sounds of his fists pounding the sides of his face and head pierce my soul and I'm holding my breath as I run to grab his hands. I can see the pain in his eyes—as if he were begging, "Please somebody stop me. I can't help it." I see the frightened faces of my other children. I feel like I can taste the blood in the air from another session of brutal, compulsive self-injury. The memories are haunting and vivid. I try to avoid them, but how do you delete pictures of the darkest time of your life? Like other parents of autistic children, I've experienced desolation, but nothing crushed me more than witnessing my son in chronic pain and psychic agony, with no end in sight.

It began when Jamey had his first immunizations at three months old, DPT and polio. Two months later, he was given a second round of the same shots. Two hours afterwards he began screaming, and it lasted for days. The pediatrician's nurse said, "Give him some Tylenol." I did, but he seemed lethargic. When I took him to the doctor the next week, he scolded me for being "overprotective" and "worrying too much." He said my son was fine. I was raised to trust doctors and other professionals—they're educated people—they're there to help.

In April of 1990 Jamey was given the MMR vaccination. Three months later, I said I didn't want the pertussis shot for him, and the doctor argued with me. I insisted I didn't like what I read about the side effects, so my son was given only the diphtheria and tetanus shot. That was the last time I let him be immunized. I knew something went wrong, but I couldn't figure out what it was. I just knew my son wasn't the same after the immunizations. It's like they took the spark out of his eyes, when he was just 16 months old.

The self-injury started when Jamey was about 23 months old. While other parents were potty training their toddlers, I was trying to stop my son from scratching pieces of skin off his face. I'd never seen anything like it. One evening I went to bed thinking life was pretty good—and then I woke up to something that changed us all forever. Jamey's scratching became face-tapping, quickly evolving to harder blows to his temples. A few weeks later, I awoke to find my son in a pool of blood. It was the beginning of a nightmare that lasted over five years, with countless futile interventions.

I look back on weeks of total chaos and mayhem. My daughter isolated herself in her room to cope with the stress. Jamey's two younger brothers became hyperactive. I was in constant crisis—poised every moment to intervene. Sometimes late at night I'd lock the bathroom door, light candles, and sink into a warm bath, weep, and pull chunks of my hair out. I hated myself for crying. In my mind it was a sign of weakness. So, instead of openly breaking down, I'd obsessively exercise, write, and isolate myself. I was drained, but I refused to let anyone see this. I was afraid we'd lose the few friends we had left if they saw how horrible our lives were. I coped with grief by remaining angry. Forget "anger management"; I needed that anger to keep me alive when everything else in me died. I prayed, attended church, and played women's soccer. All of this helped keep me from losing my mind. Besides, the anger motivated me to challenge our situation.

When I was a child, I used to cut or scratch myself under extreme stress. It was a secret. So I thought as an adult mother that God was punishing me. I felt incredibly guilty. Although SIB in disabled populations is radically different from self-mutilation in non-disabled people, I felt my son's behavior came from me somehow. Thankfully, that's not what the Bible says: "As He passed by, He saw a man blind from his birth. And his disciples asked him, 'Rabbi, who sinned, this man or his parents, that he was born blind?' Jesus answered, 'It was not that this man sinned, or his parents, but that the works of God might be made manifest in him'" (John 9: 1–3). Although it was comforting to read this verse, it didn't nullify the sense of responsibility I felt, to protect my son. Dealing with a child's compulsive SIB is too great a load for one person to carry. This behavior requires divine intervention in tangible form.

Sitting in a therapist's office or attending support meetings didn't help my son stop hitting himself. I didn't have time for phone calls and meetings with other parents who didn't know what to do either. Living with a child with compulsive SIB is like living in a war zone. Jamey's siblings were having anxiety attacks. Jamey made loud vocalizations incessantly, so nobody could concentrate on anything at home. But the love we have for him and for each other kept us together. Our family developed a sardonic sense of humor to cope with the insanity of our situation. We did everything possible to keep Jamey comfortable, healthy, and happy. His siblings helped change his diapers, fed him, and read him stories. But he kept hitting himself. It was maddening. Each family member was inwardly going crazy. We needed help.

The state system serving disabled children was sadly unequipped to deal with Jamey's compulsive SIB. Nobody could stop him from punching himself, despite a multitude of professional evaluations. We felt abandoned and alone. We had no extended family to help us. Our friends grew distant. Everything was falling apart.

My son had his first behavioral assessment when he was two years old. It was done several weeks after the teacher first reported that he was hitting himself in the classroom. The assessment was the first of dozens of reports about my son's SIB, none of which resulted in a solution.

The following are some behavioral and medical treatments we implemented during the first five years of Jamey's SIB: arm-splints, aromatherapy, chiropractic care, extinction method, helmets, hugging, hydrotherapy, massage therapy, music therapy, physical and occupational therapy, operant conditioning, re-direction, sensory integration, and speech therapy. Jamey had MRIs of the brain and spine, PET scans, and ENT (ear, nose, throat) and gastrointestinal exams. We had church elders pray over him. We tried special diets, vitamins, and herbal therapies—all of which failed to stop his SIB. Garlic supplementation and a high-fiber diet did eliminate his constipation, which was one of many antecedents to his self-injurious frenzies. But he kept hitting himself. He variously took Atarax, Clonidine, Imipramine, Luvox, Fluoxetine, Naltrexone, and Neurontin. None of these drugs reduced or stopped the SIB, and in some cases they exacerbated it. Dental and medical care became impossible. We couldn't bring our son to church or out to dinner, fearing he'd beat himself and alarm others. Finally we isolated ourselves, and lived in a state of impending doom.

Respite care was helpful, but it was never easy to find people to watch our son. There's a high turnover rate in most respite agencies, so whenever we found someone it was only for a brief time. What was worse, nobody at the agencies was trained to deal with compulsive SIBs. Finally, I asked the state Regional Center if I could become a "parent vendor." The Regional Center gives these parents a monthly stipend, according to an approved amount of respite hours for the child, and the parent finds and pays workers. It was still difficult to find people who could handle Jamey's behaviors. At one point we went through seven workers in three months.

Once, when I was alone in the car with Jamey, he began hitting himself for no apparent reason. I remember thinking, "This is hell. My son is destroying himself and I'm running out of time to help him." I sought expert advice. As soon as the experts surmised Jamey's level of care was out of their league, they wrote their reports and split. There are very few experts who are qualified to analyze and treat compulsive SIB in autistic children.

Jamey's compulsion to harm himself also took a toll on his education. "Jamey can't learn anything if he's constantly punching himself while in the classroom," I wrote to the school district. (I later learned that the school district hadn't gone through the motions of the state-required functional analysis on my son until years after the SIB started.)

In hindsight, I wish I'd known about special education and disability law the first year my son was diagnosed with autism. It took me years to navigate my way through an elaborate, often secretive system. *The truth is that schools and state agencies don't really want parents to know what is available for their child.* The state wants to control the money and resources by withholding them. This means they might lie to you. They might write fraudulent reports to justify their decisions and opinions. They might mislead you. They might intimidate you. I realize this sounds horrible, but it happens all the time.

The first time my son injured himself should've prompted the entry of his name into a database for crisis intervention at the California Department of Developmental Disabilities (this is the state agency responsible for the care and monitoring of disabled persons). *No such database exists.* Nor does one exist at the California Department of Education. Instead, my son was subjected to over five years of tedious, ineffective treatments within a loose, unmonitored bureaucracy. Had Jamey received effective behavioral intervention early, he could have been spared years of bodily injury.

In 1993 a physical therapist told me she was unable to continue therapy with Jamey due to his self-abusive behavior. For several years, he was placed in public special education classrooms, in spite of my requests for a non-public specialized placement. "We must exhaust different placements in the public school first," said one Special Education Director. "It costs a fortune to send these kids out of district." Meanwhile, my son came home from school with contusions and lacerations on his face. I threatened to sue the school for repeatedly allowing him to injure himself while in their care; I should have done so. The last straw: Jamey returned home from school with welts on his face and head, and the school couldn't explain how they got there. Finally, I discovered I could request a "Fair Hearing" with the California Department of Education. I had to convince the state mediator that the public school setting wasn't the best environment for my son. It was the first time I formally advocated for him, and it wouldn't be the last. In fact, parents of severely autistic children must prepare themselves for a lifetime of parental advocacy.

In 1994 Jamey was placed at a non-public school in San Diego where he received one-on-one behavioral and educational support that reduced the physical injuries. But it didn't stop the behavior. Finally, in 1995, after extensive research, I discovered a controversial behavioral treatment known as *skin-stimulus therapy*. At first I thought it was bizarre, but the research I read showed it was an effective and safe therapy for autistic children who were unresponsive to conventional therapies and "at high risk for continually injuring themselves." Well, that fit my son's profile to a tee.

I wondered why no one had ever told me about this therapy. I found out when I asked the San Diego Regional Center to support it. "That's an aversive therapy," said their psychologist. "If you try to get it, we'll call Child Protective Services," said another employee. I was disappointed and confused by their response. Apparently, it was okay for the Regional Center to send a plethora of psychologists into our home, all of whom failed to treat Jamey's SIB, but it wasn't okay for me to consider a therapy that could actually protect him from further injury. It made no sense. Ironically, it was the school and state systems that endangered my son's health and safety by failing to protect him.

"It appears some people are opposed to my son's medically prescribed device because they're uncomfortable with it," I told the psychologist. "This shows a callous disregard for my son's needs." The real shocker: most people who opposed the skin-stimulus therapy didn't know my son and hadn't read the research on the therapy. They'd never met him, seen his injuries, nor spoken to me. Instead, these opponents based their opinions on abstractions and subjective prejudice, and willfully ignored the facts pertaining to my son. To add insult to injury, Protection and Advocacy and the Regional Center (which are funded by the California Department of Developmental Services) refused to support the therapy. "We're philosophically opposed to this treatment," said one of their attorneys. "If we advocate for this treatment, it will set a precedent for other children to use it."

The controversial therapy is known as SIBIS (Self-Injurious Behavior Inhibitor System). It runs off a nine-volt battery. It's a small FDA-approved device for treatment-resistant SIB. You need a prescription to use it at home or in school. It delivers a brief, mild skin stimulus that feels like the prick of a needle from a vaccination shot. According to research, SIBIS could protect Jamey from continual bodily injury. Why should anyone want to deny my son an effective behavioral treatment? I was stunned to learn the "anti-aversive" crowd ignored research showing SIBIS to be effective, and sought to vilify parents who used it.

Thank God for our Kaiser Permanente neurologist. He wrote a prescription for the device. This allowed us to use it at home. This neurologist was concerned that if Jamey continued hitting himself he would fracture his skull or cause brain hemorrhaging. Jamey also has epilepsy, so continual head punches place him in a higher risk category. But those facts didn't change the doctrinaire thinking of SIBIS opponents. They downplayed and minimized Jamey's condition. It appeared they were willing to sacrifice my son's health to protect their hyper-vigilant, misguided belief system. This illuminated a dark and disturbing truth about some top officials working in state organizations for the disabled—*they aren't there for the children.*

After SIBIS, Jamey's behavior was nearly extinguished at home. But he was still hitting himself at school, and California's Hughes Bill made it illegal for him to use SIBIS therapy in his educational program. (The Hughes Bill is a great idea, but it's written as if children with unresponsive, compulsive self-injury don't exist.) I argued that inconsistent use of a behavioral therapy jeopardizes progress. "I agree it makes no behavioral sense to inconsistently apply the therapy across settings, but we just can't support this," one said.

People say God works in mysterious ways. He did. I received an educational waiver to allow my son to wear his medically prescribed device at school. There was an immediate reduction in his behaviors within the first month of SIBIS. The aides and teacher didn't have to hold his hands down while he tried to bite his fingers or tried to pummel his nose. Jamey could focus on learning! That didn't matter to the SIBIS opponents. It didn't matter to the Regional Center either. San Diego Regional Center didn't like the educational waiver. In fact, they continued to deny my son access to his therapy in his after-school program. So, Jamey would use the device at home and in school, and then he would walk fifty feet to his San Diego Regional Center-funded after school program, and he couldn't use his behavioral treatment. According to Regional Center staff, had Jamey needed an insulin shot, which is also painful, that would be okay. But a device causing no more pain than an insulin shot that's designed to stop him from pummeling his skull to shreds—that wasn't okay. In 2001, after years of requesting that Regional Center support the use of SIBIS in order to maintain consistency across settings, the director wrote me a letter that stated, "The San Diego Regional Center generally does not support behavior modification that involves pain and trauma... I encourage you to work with the Regional Center Interdisciplinary Team to address your son's needs."

He obviously hadn't taken the time to review my son's history. He hadn't examined the attempts I made to meet with Regional Center employees, all of whom were vehemently opposed to my son's only effective therapy. My response to the director was, "San Diego Regional Center has denied my son the same advocacy, protection, and services afforded other disabled children, due to your ongoing philosophical judgments and failure to respect the individual needs of my child." I never heard from him again. Ironically, a behavioral psychologist hired by the Regional Center wrote a favorable report about Jamey's SIBIS therapy. But Regional Center employees ignored his report and recommendations.

What I regret: as an inexperienced young mother of a newly diagnosed autistic toddler, I waited too long to speak up for my son. It wasn't until a few years after he was diagnosed that I vowed never to make that mistake again. I trusted the professionals to tell me my child's rights and direct me toward appropriate resources. But they didn't tell me; I found out through other parents. I trusted the school district to provide appropriate supports. It didn't. I had to research and fight for everything my child needed. I trusted the state to monitor my child's needs. It didn't. I had to remind them about my son. I waited for doctors to tell me the results of exams. They didn't call. I had to call them to find out. As a parent of an autistic child, you are the first and only line of defense against a system that will lose your child in a file cabinet. Your child will be a faceless number on tired pieces of paper or computer programs unless you make his or her needs known, over and over.

There are no quick fixes for compulsive SIB. There are no fancy tricks or treatments. You can't simply medicate a child and expect the problem to disappear. Inept professionals want quick fixes. They want to do a drive-by analysis of your child, get paid big bucks, and disappear. A truly qualified professional will spend months examining your child and analyzing comprehensive data. But in the meantime the behaviors must be stopped. It's an all-out war, and the last therapist standing is usually the parent. Every day is a crisis for a child who repeatedly self-injures. It's not behavior that is helped by endless pontification—it requires swift, aggressive intervention.

SIBIS was the most effective treatment for our son's SIB. After seven years, his behaviors are manageable without it. Occasionally, he still hits himself, but he doesn't exhibit the brutal, compulsive behaviors seen in the dark pre-SIBIS days. SIBIS was a long-term treatment, which gradually increased his self-control. It took time and commitment. He had no self-control prior to skin-stimulus therapy. Most beneficial: the skin-stimulus therapy allowed us to introduce other treatments he didn't respond to prior to using SIBIS.

I strongly believe the greatest barrier to effective treatments is the lack of commitment displayed by federal and state officials responsible for the care and monitoring of autistic children with severe behaviors. The ugly truth is that most self-injurious autistic people are heavily medicated, and hidden from public view in group homes and institutions. Top officials don't want the public to know about autistic persons placed in 24-hour restraints, forced into arm splints and helmets, and given chemical lobotomies. The anti-aversive crowd doesn't want the public to know what goes on in county and state facilities serving the disabled. It casts a shadow on their "let's close down the institutions" and "positive behavioral intervention only" policies. The bottom line is this: if you ignore or downplay dangerous behaviors in the autistic population, it nurtures apathy and breeds additional damaging health issues in the entire disabled population. To ignore research showing the effectiveness of skin-stimulus therapy (in the rare cases that warrant this intervention) is tantamount to child abuse, and violates the innate desire of parents to protect their children. If county and state officials have authority to undermine a parent's right to provide critical care for their child, we are living in dishonorable times.

After 13 years of analyzing and observing SIB, I've learned to anticipate everything possible that is, or could be, an antecedent to this behavior. You must study the self-injurious child. Learn how they think and feel. Truth is independent of belief. It doesn't matter what others believe about your child, the truth is based on who your child is.

I designed the following to help parents of autistic children suffering from compulsive SIB.

How to provide comprehensive preliminary analysis of an autistic child with SIB

An analysis is not merely a description of the self-injurious individual or the re-written contents of history reports—rather, it includes an examination of all medical, behavioral, and environmental issues pertaining to that child or adult. It entails interviewing direct caregivers and parents who can share information on unique aspects of the individual's life. Then, case analysis evolves into making clear connections to theories and research on SIB and applying them to the individual settings.

Record types of SIB (describe exactly what happens). Don't use vague terminology. "Johnny has self-injurious behavior" is not sufficient.

1. Punching self

2. Slapping self

3. Biting self

4. Pulling own hair

5. Body slamming

6. Head banging

7. Cutting or hitting self w/object

8. Burning self

Frequency of SIB

1. Daily

2. How often

Degrees of SIB

1. *Mild* (soft slaps to face or head—no marks whatsoever)

2. *Moderate* (slaps to face with red marks—mild bruising, no deep bruising or cuts visible)

3. *Severe* (SIB causes loss of hair, leaves deep purple bruises, cuts, or scratches)

Type of SIB					Behavioral Interventions Used				
Frequency of SIB	Degree of SIB	Duration of SIB	Times when normally occurs	Antecedents to SIB	Pharmaceutical therapies used	Special diets tried	Nutritional therapies tried	Alternative therapies used	Medical/dental evaluations completed

4.   *Life-threatening* (e.g. severe punches to head, knocking out teeth, chronic self-induced vomiting, putting pencils or other sharp objects inside ears)

Duration of SIB

1.   How long does episode last before complete cessation?

2.   When does the behavior occur?

3.   Keep a daily chart.

4.   Evaluate weekly.

Antecedents to SIB

1.   What specific event(s) happened before SIB occurred?

2.   Where did it happen?

3.   What was going on around the child?

Behavioral Interventions Used

1.   List every behavioral therapy tried.

2.   What were the results of the therapy?

3.   How long was it tried?

4.   Were there any other therapies used in conjunction?

Remember, a non-verbal child, or one with difficulty communicating, will not tell you what's wrong. *You have to investigate.* The top five underlying medical conditions most likely to cause pain and agitation:

1.   Stomach/digestive problems, or anything unusual about digestion

2.   Ear, nose, and throat problems

3.   Headaches

4.   Toothaches

5.   Sprains or sore muscles

Top five environmental conditions most likely to cause agitation

1. Loud noises

2. Unfamiliar people

3. No safety zone available

4. Visual disturbances (pictures or posters can be upsetting—or seeing things out of order; flashing lights might be a factor, or fluorescent lighting)

5. Transitions to unfamiliar places

Warning about getting help: some dirty tricks schools and states play

School and state officials might inflate a child's progress or exaggerate achievements to downplay needs. Be forewarned: this is a dirty trick to thwart parents from seeking additional services.

- Schools tell parents they must immunize children. That's a lie. Parents have the right to refuse to give their children vaccinations for philosophical, religious, or medical reasons. It's a highly personal decision—not one that should be forced by the state.

- Regional Centers are notorious for not telling parents what resources are available.

- Regional Centers don't want parents to write a child's needs on the IEP (Individualized Education Program). The IEP is a legal document, so they avoid writing requests on it. They prefer to have meetings and "talk about things." This translates into informal, idle babbling that results in very little for your child—and wastes your time. If you know exactly what your child needs, fight for it. Don't get sucked into attending mediations or having phone conferences. There's a time to talk and a time to take action. Parents should decide when that is.

- School and state officials use circular reasoning and diversionary tactics to stall parents seeking services for their

children. The biggest stall tactic: going to meetings, where
nothing is accomplished.

- School and state officials may attempt to shame or scold
  parents for seeking services. Confront them when they do.

Out-of-home placements

Few parents choose to place their child in an out-of-home facility. The
reality is that they're compelled to consider placement after years of
chronic stress and lack of in-home supports. They're burned out and
confused. They're overwhelmed by the barrage of duties associated with
raising a child with intensive needs. They're tired of playing the games
favored by school and state officials. They're concerned about the effects
on their other children. They're on the verge of divorce or insanity. Their
cries for help were most likely neglected for too long. Sometimes they seek
placement for other reasons, but most families I've known sought placement as a last resort, with their backs to the wall.

Ironically, after placing a child in a residential program, the Department of Developmental Services sends parents a bill. They nail parents with
a monthly charge without having afforded the parents the right to receive
the same monies allocated to out-of-home placements. It's really bizarre
how that works. In short, the state will pay a group home $5000 a month
for your child, but you, as a parent, will never be offered that amount or any
other amount to maintain your child in your home. You also won't be
afforded the same access to resources for your child that the state agencies
have. To get anything, you must go through the Regional Centers. That's a
real problem—the Regional Centers control most of the funding and
resources available to families with autistic children. Why not give parents a
monthly stipend based on their child's needs, and let parents go directly to
a state resource agency to purchase services? Why does the state play parent
to our children? Some parents don't want the responsibility of finding, pur-
chasing, and monitoring their child's services, and that's fine; let a special
unit handle those parents. The rest of us, who want to be the parents no
matter what, should be supported in our efforts to do the best for our
children in their own home. It should be a personal choice.

After 13 years of raising a severely autistic child with SIB, I had no
choice. My family was shattered by years of bungled supports and willful
neglect from corrupt state agencies. Ironically, the sprawling bureaucracy

serving the disabled controls over one billion dollars a year, but still manages to consistently fail families with disabled children. It makes you wonder where the money goes.

It's not easy sifting through conflicting media stories about autism. Parents must use caution and discernment when evaluating therapies for their child. Do lots of research. Gather concrete evidence. Be careful how you spend your time and energy. Don't rely on speculation or case studies about other autistic children—study your own child. Try dietary and nutritional treatments if you can—consider trying the casein/gluten free diet, the ketogenic diet, the specific carbohydrate diet, etc. Consider alternative therapies like cranio-sacral therapy, acupuncture, and occupational and physical therapy, including sensory integration. They're not as invasive as pharmaceutical therapies, and they don't inflict damage; drugs can.

Over the years, I learned to match treatments to specific challenges related to my son's disabilities. For instance, his autism, epilepsy, and compulsive SIBs warrant particular dietary and nutritional interventions, but I wanted them to complement each other, so I designed a high-protein, high-fiber, high-good fat, low-sugar, moderate carbohydrate diet tailored to his needs. I advocated including this on his IEP. It wasn't easy. The school demanded a medical prescription for the diet I spent months creating. I'm his mother; it was insulting to think I needed a doctor's note to feed my child healthy foods, but I got it. Jamey's diet is carefully crafted to counter-attack fluctuating and complex antecedents to his behaviors. In my opinion, an unhealthy child is an uncomfortable child. If my son is uncomfortable for any reason, he hits himself. Staying healthy entails a lifetime of data analysis, and of monitoring behavioral, dental, environmental, educational, dietary, medical, and nutritional needs. It is an important proactive intervention to compulsive self-injury. Who will do this, but a loving caregiver or parent?

The best advice I can give other parents is this: do your own research. Don't be bullied by medical, school, or state officials. They aren't invested in your child's health and welfare. You are the experts. Keep records. Get everything in writing. Document everything that happens in your child's life. Never give up. Fight for your child's right to live a healthy and safe life.

NINETEEN

Irina Lobkovitz

Henry was brought home from the hospital with diarrhea, but what did I know as a new mother? I didn't even know if I was right to keep reporting it, but eventually the pediatrician agreed that blood in the stool was not normal. He prescribed sulfasuccidine, boiled milk (four minutes, no sugar), scraped raw apple, and ripe banana.

My young husband and I felt helpless when our baby cried (not whimpered) for 15 out of 30 hours straight. He wasn't breastfed very long, as he was a "lazy sucker," and my nipples were raw and bleeding. How I wished that La Leche League had a presence in San Diego!

By six months, the pediatrician's colleague thought Henry was 13 months, so he'd thrived, in spite of his eczema and my clumsy mothering. He didn't crawl, walked at one year, could read at three and a half, and spent a lot of time taking things apart. I fed him on Gerber's baby food and strained meat. Music and records fascinated him and still do. Tubes and radios: he knew them all by number (in electronics, a tube is a device used to amplify, switch, or modify a signal by controlling the movement of electrons). With his 18-months-younger brother, he learned to bicycle, swim, and dance (sort of!).

At age four, Henry adapted to my going back to work as a technical writer. The very dear Chinese/Hawaiian lady I split my paycheck with (one-third to Uncle Sam, one-third to Ivy) had two girls about the same age as my boys, and her Navy husband became a second father to them.

In time, the boys transferred to a midtown school with the city's first gifted classes, and they learned to ride the bus. After-school Natural History Museum classes were a blessing for all of us.

In high school, Henry was known for his math and science prowess; his brother was a dutiful and adequate scholar, but never equal to Henry. The brothers fought a lot; my younger son, being wily, was glad to see the favored eldest blamed for acts he himself instigated.

On the advice of a family friend, we sent the boys to Berkeley instead of Cal Tech for college; it seemed to be a clear choice for Henry in the interest of socializing him. It was a mistake; a community college would have accomplished socializing without exposure to the turmoil of the 1960s at the big campus. For Henry, there was no more cello or playing with the orchestra; in his freshman year, he ran a student radio station, made wine, and helped out at the free (freak) clinic. Without a car, he tasted "Berzerkeley" street life and the world of sex, even arranging the funeral of a middle-aged girlfriend who died of a stroke. He ran an urban farm in the backyard of the house where he lived on the main thoroughfare, Nash Street, and he abandoned the pursuit of his Master of Science degree in biochemistry.

When we realized what was happening, we sent his brother to bring him home. They came back with a trailer full of chickens and rabbits that moved into our empty sand-bottomed swimming pool. The feral rooster, a handsome bird, soon brought complaints from the neighbors for his early morning vocalizing, and the reproductive rate of the rabbits sealed their doom.

The boys' dad, probably an Asperger's type himself (neither he nor our son has ever received a diagnosis) is an engineer with a keen interest in horse racing and poker. He got Henry a job in the Safety Department where he worked, a new department since the OSHA (Occupational Safety and Health Administration). Henry worked in the aircraft industry for 13 years, until a general lay-off.

By then Henry had lived at four addresses in the neighborhood and trashed them all. His lifestyle wasn't tidy. On the plus side, his cute but elderly girlfriend, a retired musician, dancer, librarian, and divorced mother of eight, convinced him to have his hernia operated on, introduced him to acting as a guide at a nearby park, and got him to participate on the board of a spiritualist chapel.

His main joy in life is downloading early ethnic jazz. He chooses not to be available by phone, and uses my computer when speed is needed. He's usually very careful with his money—in fact stingy—but depends on family to help him out with practical problems. Only the threat of disinheritance brought him to enrollment in a Health Maintenance Organization, which he pays for but refuses to make use of. He thinks he knows best about diets. He avoids family interaction unless a firm demand is issued. He is our computer guru, and loves to play "professor" as he explains things to us. Any family inheritance, whatever that may be, is in the form of a trust.

Lessons learned

- A relationship with a child with a disability is not so different from any parent–child relationship.

- Be specific in criticism—give instructions, give examples, use key phrases. Go easy on punishment; it breeds resentment. Let the child experience consequences, pro and con.

- Teach your child how to prepare meals, do laundry, fill out forms, and how to behave in different situations. Consider exposure to ways to perform in front of people, as in junior theater, debating, etc.

- Teach First Aid, personal hygiene, safety practices. Teach about money as a responsibility.

- Train for orderliness, organization, and care of belongings; material possessions don't seem to be important to autistics.

- Expose your child to varied experiences to counter their tendency to perseverate (tendency to repeat or prolong). Have friends of all ages and types. Experiment with art, swimming, judo or karate, bicycling, pets. Encourage acceptance of individual differences; project appreciation of normalcy, in the sense of avoiding an attitude of expecting special handling. A parent should monitor teacher/child interactions and try to make the best of the learning experience.

- Teach concern for others, but instruct in self-defense.

- Provide a quiet place for reading, study, or just to be alone.

- Teach the concept of priorities, as a way toward satisfying a person's wants and needs.

- Motivation is all-important; rewards work! Parental influence can be eroded if praise is withheld; once gone, there is no way back, except as an accommodation.

- Parents must reorder their expectations as the autistic or ADD child matures. Be aware of up-to-date research, but realize that when your child is an adult, he or she makes his/her own decisions.

TWENTY

Kristin Zhivago

Michael is 47 going on five. He used to be going on three, but now he's five, because he speaks in full sentences. This is a fairly new development, starting with ear retraining about fifteen years ago.

It wasn't until we retrained his hearing that we realized he'd spent most of his life unable to hear consonants. If we said, "Hi, Michael, how are you today?" he heard: "Hi, Ile, how are ou uay?" This is what he would repeat back to us—just as he heard it. And we would invariably say, "What?"

For most of his life, Michael was stuck in a one-way communication hell, where he heard us, then repeated what we said to him exactly as he heard it, only to find us perplexed. This was frustrating for him, to say the least. So when we did understand him, he would be gleeful, and he would repeat that phrase over and over, so glad that we'd connected.

After we retrained his hearing, he could finally hear high-frequency sounds, such as s, t, and f. He started to teach himself to talk using consonants. Now instead of saying, "Wanna go wal?" he can say, "I want to go for a walk, please." "Where are we going?" "What's her name?" He is still having trouble with the 's' sound, because it involves an invisible trick: you must know that the tongue has to be pulled back from behind the teeth. Try showing someone where your tongue is when you say the letter 's' and you will see what I mean: your teeth are in the way. Also, years of seizure medications have given Michael a tongue that's a bit swollen. But he continues to work on it, and has mastered a lispy 's' that gets the point across.

After his ear retraining, I remember we had a "Helen Keller moment." We were taking one of our long drives, and we found ourselves in an agricultural area in the eastern area of San Diego County. We were driving past miles of irrigation ditches. Michael loves puddles, and loves to slam his foot down in any puddle he passes, spraying water all around. So he often points out creeks and other water. As we went past these irrigation ditches, he kept saying, "Wa-cr" as he always did, and I kept correcting him. "Honey, it's Wa-Ter," I said, over and over. He kept watching my face, and listening, and trying, and finally he got it, and was thrilled. It goes without saying that "wa-ter" was the most popular word for the rest of the trip.

We always knew that Michael had sensitivity to low-frequency sounds. Even as an infant, passing motorcycles and airplanes caused him to put both hands on his ears. Now we understand that all appliances, even when they're turned off, "growl" at him. (Turn off your TV, put your ear up against it, and you will hear that "hum." That "hum" is very, very loud for people like Michael.)

In fact, he calls telephone poles "monsters" because the transformers on the poles emit a low-frequency hum that, for him, can be very frightening. I remember one day in particular, we were taking a long walk, and hadn't got back to our car yet until after sunset. The growling from the telephone poles along the road made him desperate to get into a car—any car—so we could drive away from the danger. Once we understand the sensitivity of their "wiring," we can start to decode the way they're acting.

I first became aware of the hearing issues while watching an interview of "Georgie" and her mother. Georgie went through the ear retraining as described in the book, *Hearing Equals Behavior*, by Guy Berard, MD. Her mother wrote a book about Georgie's transformation from a petrified child to a well-functioning adult, thanks to the retraining, called *Sound of a Miracle: A Child's Triumph Over Autism*.

It was difficult to find anyone who could conduct the ear retraining properly (its formal name is Auditory Integration Therapy), but we did. First she tested Michael for sensitivities by putting earphones on his head (not something he wanted to do!), then playing sounds that would cause him to react in some way (sometimes very violently). But she was sensitive to his facial expressions and reactions, and we already knew that low-frequency "rumbling" sounds were a problem, so she didn't have to subject him to that particular test.

Michael then listened to filtered music through headphones, twice a day for ten days, for half an hour each session. And yes, he had to be convinced that it was the right thing for him to do. But he calmed down after a while, because the music was filtered to specifically exclude the sounds he found hurtful. He got so he could finally hear the high-frequency sounds that he'd never heard before, and thus began his journey into the world of hearing, and then saying, consonants.

It wasn't until he'd mastered some of the consonants that we realized what a difference the ear retraining had made, and that he'd never been able to repeat what we said because he simply couldn't hear everything.

We've experimented with various other things for Michael, including "Cell Food," (through LuminaHealth.com), which helps his mental alertness, the B supplements that Dr. Bernie Rimland recommends, DMG, and something called Reconcostat, which adjusts his pH balance; these have provided some benefit. But none of them compares to the change in his life due to the ear retraining, with one exception: Wendy Smith.

Wendy Smith was the supervisor of Michael's house for many years, part of the Home of Guiding Hands in Lakeside, California. Wendy has her own autistic son, and so is particularly aware of how autistic people think. But she also has a unique talent for creating programs that help the autistic person grow and develop. She's done a fantastic job of training the staff at Michael's house, so they understand how to approach him, how to help him deal with frustration, how to help him learn, and to do the right thing. Michael has blossomed in that environment, where the staff apply consistent guidance, day in and day out. The other staff members at the Home of Guiding Hands, including new supervisors at his house, have also been fantastic—a true blessing. Michael continues to improve, and is basically a happy person.

TWENTY-ONE

Sue Swezey

H ow did John get to be 40 and bald? And for that matter, when did I become a senior citizen?

Like it or not, our children age, and we (perhaps faster) along with them. When John was little, I used to think that if only "they" knew how difficult it was to cope with an autistic child, "they" would do something about it. Not until years later did I realize that "they" turn out to be simply other parents, those who share the same experiences, and must help each other if anything is ultimately to change for the better. By sharing our stories, we hope others might avoid our pitfalls and benefit from our successes.

A shaky start

John was a beautiful, healthy baby, a relief after a prolonged delivery and an early scare: I was exposed to German measles six weeks into pregnancy. I was given the standard treatment of the time, a gamma globulin injection, and was somewhat reassured by reading Dr. Spock, whose best-selling baby manual stated that only 1 in 200 babies were born with deformities. Despite this underlying concern, we were eager for John's birth. After all, we were graduates of Red Cross Preparation for Parents Classes—we knew how to bathe a rubber doll. When John finally arrived, even if he slept little and screamed a lot, we felt we could cope—at least barely.

After three months the screaming subsided and John became an adorable, happy infant. True, with both nursing and formula we were often "bathed in barf," but our pediatrician observed that John lacked the mechanism to know when to stop eating, not a matter for concern. At one year he had four halting words, and was lively and energetic.

But at 18 months, as other toddlers in the neighborhood began to talk, John became less and less communicative. By two he was either tantrumming or bouncing, and bed-rocking with manic glee. By three he'd been banished from the local babysitting co-op. He was hyperactive and miserable—and I was pregnant again.

The downward path

Specialists were hard to come by, and it was not until after the birth of our daughter that we began rounds of fruitless appointments: hearing tests (normal), weekly speech therapy (unproductive), and socialization (disastrous). At the urging of neighbors who had great faith in the virtue of co-op nurseries, John was enrolled in a nearby preschool. By a quirk of fate, the nursery already contained an autistic child—the only other one in our town of 30,000—who quickly became the aggressor to John, as the screaming victim. Overwhelmed by this dynamic duo, the teacher collapsed from exhaustion mid-year and asked John to leave, the first of many expulsions.

John began to collect labels: hyperactive, neurologically handicapped, emotionally disturbed, autistic-like, "troubled" (this from a therapist who didn't believe in labels so invented his own). I acquired a label, too: Refrigerator Mother.

Few programs were available in the late 1960s, but family therapy was a requirement for all of them, in the tradition of "Can This Marriage Be Saved?" As a result, I was assigned a social worker from the Family Service Agency, a Viennese man who'd narrowly escaped the Holocaust and who felt deep compassion for victims of concentration camps. He was also a Freudian and a Bettelheim adherent. No sooner had the therapist introduced himself than he took one look at our engaging 18-month-old daughter and declared that, if she'd been our first child, she would be as disturbed as John. He said John was like the children in the death camps, whose cries were forcibly stifled for safety. When I assured him that John's cries were definitely not stifled (impossible to do), he then decided that John must have observed flagrant sex (rather amusing, as tantrums in the background were something of a turn-off). If not us, he replied, then our sitter (poor dear, over 200 pounds—she might have wished!).

In an odd way, this line of reasoning proved helpful; I realized then with absolute clarity that whatever our faults, John's problems came from within himself. We were anxious to learn how to work with him, but were told repeatedly that *we* were the ones who needed fixing; we'd already done enough damage. Or, rather, *I* had, since Bettelheim had already revealed, by positing the now infamous "Refrigerator Mother" theory of autism, that mothers were to blame.

When he was six, John acquired the autism label and began a steady decline in a series of programs designed for the emotionally disturbed, where his "psychosis" was uninterrupted and allowed to run its course. The only programs available were far from home, so isolated families in our county banded together; I used to think my epitaph might read: "She Organized Car Pools." As was standard practice at the time, professionals recommended that we institutionalize John and lead a normal life ourselves—whatever that might be. In the early 1970s, 95 percent of all known autistic people in the US lived in institutions, with far too many *Snake Pit* (a 1948 movie about a scary state-run mental hospital) scenarios. Our child was on the brink.

By age ten, John had hit bottom. He used only a few words, most of them echolalic (repeating what someone else says); his single meaningful communication was "No!" His only achievements were counting to ten and writing the alphabet, often backwards. He was marginally toilet-trained, slept little, and screamed a lot. We had exhausted all possibilities, and ourselves.

In retrospect, there were four factors in John's early years that contributed to lifetime deficits:

1. *Rubella.* The 1963 rubella epidemic caused a blip in the incidence of autism; the disease can affect the developing brain. The gamma globulin shot I was given was later discontinued for rubella exposure because it could mask symptoms without preventing the disease. After the rubella outbreak, research

determined that a fetus could contract rubella independent of the mother; I do not have rubella antibodies, but John does. However, since he also had the vaccine when it first became available, we'll never know for sure if he had rubella in utero, but it still remains the most likely suspect. Ironically, today's MMR vaccine might have protected John but is itself suspect as a possible factor in the current autism epidemic.

2.   *Food sensitivities and digestive problems.* Early digestive problems should have been a clue that something was amiss, if not to me then certainly to our pediatrician. It's likely that I was eating foods while pregnant and nursing to which John was highly allergic. As he became more autistic, he refused most foods and probably suffered a degree of malnutrition. Meals were a struggle, and it was not until his eleventh year that I acquired the knowledge and skill to enforce an appropriate diet.

3.   *Lack of early intervention.* While I talked, read, and sang to John as an infant, his mind just wasn't able to process verbal communication normally. As his autism progressed, he missed much of the normal sequence of language development. I had vaguely heard about behavior modification, but the technique was strongly criticized as being too much like animal training; anyway, we weren't supposed to interfere with his "psychosis." John was allowed to regress just when vigorous intervention would have been of the greatest benefit.

4.   *Isolation.* When John was an infant, the autism ratio was about 4:10,000. No parent organization existed in our area. There was only one other autistic child in town, the little boy who bullied John at the co-op nursery. With so little public knowledge of autism, friends and family alike regarded John as disturbed. Understandably, neighbors didn't want their children to play with him, and we were never invited to gatherings with other families.

The turning point

Only one chance remained for John; it was a new school that attempted to *teach* autistic children, a practice then untried in the US. We were cautioned against this school, The Morgan Center, as it lacked funding, had no playground, and was certain to fold. I'd seen a video of the program, and I felt that the smiling, capable children on the tape did not share the same problems as my son. When Morgan Center's Director Louise Emerson first observed John, he turned and ran. She said, "He looks like one of ours." I knew (or thought I knew) he wasn't.

John's previous, psychiatrically oriented program stated that "his psychosis is progressing to the point where, unless major inroads are made, it will become irreversible." Louise Emerson snorted in response: "Major Inroads was one of our founders!" We enrolled John at Morgan Center, moved closer to the school, and waited for the inevitable tantrums. Months later, we were still waiting. After five months I realized with a shock that John was beginning to use language to communicate. Even more astounding, he was smiling and laughing. Surely a miracle had occurred. The true test came when we flew from California to Chicago to visit my family; for the first time we could take the same airline both ways and not worry that they'd remember our screaming child from the outbound flight!

What caused such a quick and dramatic change in John? He'd found the right program. At that time there were 15 students enrolled at Morgan Center, with one teacher for every child. Every minute was filled with activity, keeping the children's attention constantly focused. Teachers were alert for anything approximating a correct response, promptly rewarding it with praise, and sometimes food. There were no negative consequences, no "time-outs," no punishments. The physiological aspects of autism were addressed, with gross- and fine-motor training and sensory integration therapy. Perhaps most important, the program was based on communication; the children received daily doses of individual language therapy, with all the teachers reinforcing language goals. The difference between this approach and some of today's ABA programs is that the emphasis was on learning and on positive reinforcement, not on behavior as such. When the child's interest was caught and he began to make sense of the outer world, much problem behavior disappeared of its own accord.

Food for thought

We'd reached the end of our rope shortly before John began at Morgan Center. We'd explored every conventional path, but in California in the early 1970s, the unconventional was burgeoning: at the urging of a friend, I surreptitiously consulted a psychic. Even with the dawning of the Age of

Aquarius, I knew that no rational, college-educated person would stoop so low, but I was desperate. Rebellion was the hallmark of the era, and I was rebelling against the prevailing abysmal ignorance of the medical/psychiatric establishment.

More than thirty years later, I've not quite recovered from that initial encounter. Autism had scarcely been identified, yet this woman, Bella the psychic, seemed to understand John inside and out. She rattled on for hours about possible approaches (some *really* far-out) to take with him and made a statement that seemed especially unlikely: "There will be more and more of these special children coming in, and we must learn how to understand and work with them before they overwhelm us." This was in 1972, when the incidence of autism was statistically insignificant. Her prediction has proved all too true.

Several of Bella's recommendations were about diet; she seemed to have a sense of what John lacked, and was especially concerned about allergies. After John started Morgan Center, one of the staff privately taught us behavior management techniques to train him to accept new foods. I found a pediatrician who specialized in food allergies, and we started on a rigorous allergy-reduction diet. It took a year to identify foods to which John was sensitive (mainly corn and dairy, plus refined sugar, additives, and food coloring), but the diet was ultimately successful in eliminating the need for behavior-altering medications.

The angst of adolescence

Prior to entering Morgan Center, three other programs required John to take medications for behavior. In each case, the initial benefit of the drug soon wore off, leaving side effects that exceeded the original problem. The worst was Thorazine, one of a family of medications developed to control patients in state hospitals. Thorazine was prescribed by the program that didn't want to interfere with his "psychosis"; their only intervention for emerging behavioral issues was to raise the dose. Alarmed by John's increasing lethargy and depression, I discreetly weaned him off Thorazine, with supplemental doses of B-complex vitamins concealed in applesauce. When the program found out, they acted as if I'd jeopardized his future, if not his life.

While John made great strides after entering Morgan Center, his behavioral problems didn't disappear. During the first few years he would have been classified as ADHD, if that label had been invented yet, but at least he was happy and hyper, not sad and hyper. We tried a brief course of Ritalin, which only made him somber. Morgan Center preferred to administer coffee, which worked as well. However, at the onset of adolescence stimulants ceased to sedate, and had the opposite effect. Fortunately, the change in diet at this point made further medication unnecessary.

A far worse problem was the onset of seizures at age 11. I memorized from Dr. Spock's baby manual that seizures are frightening but do no lasting damage (not entirely true, as we later discovered). John developed full-blown *grand mal*; the fire department became a frequent visitor. We experimented with meds for ten years, but blessedly, John left seizures behind with adolescence—with one exception. After 19 seizure-free years, a sudden weight gain caused his Dilantin level to dip too rapidly, and the resulting seizure astonished us all. Strict adherence to diet and frequent blood tests since that incident have controlled the problem, we hope. Alas, "You never outgrow your need for milk"—anticonvulsants.

John's school career roughly coincided with adolescence, starting at ten and ending at age 22. In retrospect, this period had its distinct challenges, some of which still face autistic teens and their families:

- *Medications.* In the early 1970s I was appalled at the heavy doses of behavior-altering medication prescribed for autistic children and adolescents. A friend gave me an outdated copy of the Physician's Desk Reference (PDR), which many of us shared in an effort to understand side effects. Thanks to the internet, today's parents are much better informed, though in my view behavioral medications are still prescribed far too often. I feel strongly that dietary changes and biomedical interventions should be tried before resorting to medication for behavior control.

- *Diet.* Even in a good program, John would be increasingly hard to manage without changes in his diet. Since blood tests for allergies can produce inconsistent results, an elimination diet is more accurate in pinpointing food sensitivities. It's also a lot of work, with a daily regimen of foods and a lot of recordkeeping. Eliminating dietary allergens and treating seasonal allergies have done wonders to improve his behavior and outlook, and are well worth the effort.

- *Seizures.* British researcher Dr. Michael Rutter once stated that low-functioning autistic children were likely to develop seizures in adolescence. John had company, as nearly all his peers at Morgan Center had seizures in their teens. One theory held that the developing brain, unable to process input, was starved for stimulation and created its own electrical hyperactivity. Another theory suspected a progressive loss of nerve myelination, with hormonal changes in adolescence precipitating seizure activity. Whatever the cause, John's seizures were severe enough to result in an increasing degree of retardation. We were fortunate that a low dose of Dilantin was eventually effective, though today he must be continually monitored for long-term side effects, such as liver damage and osteoporosis. The current tidal wave of autistic children seem to exhibit fewer seizure disorders in their teens; perhaps early intervention or biomedical treatments have made the difference, or maybe they simply have a different form of autism.

The shock of adulthood

Louise Emerson always maintained that autistic adults were ready to blossom, and in 1985 Morgan Center created an Adult Program, just at the moment when many of the students became too old for school funding. The legal start of adulthood was then the end of a student's 22nd year, as established by PL 94-142, the Education for the Handicapped Act of 1975 (now the IDEA law); at that time, students were allowed to complete the school year in which they turned 22. Today, adulthood officially begins at the instant of the 22nd birthday, causing the removal of many students from their programs mid-year, with great personal and family disruption.

Even in a familiar place with familiar staff, John's transition to adulthood was difficult. The school with an individualized program that he was used to now became a workshop with large-group activities. The school had provided ability grouping, but the adults in the new workshop program were lumped together. Some could read and do academics; others were at preschool level. Some had excellent fine-motor skills, useful for workshop tasks; others were apraxic, with little motor control. Some were quite verbal, others nonverbal. But they all had two things in common: they were autistic, and they didn't like change.

John's reaction was at first perplexing. During his school years a favorite leisure activity was building with Lego; he constructed elaborate models of houses with intricate working parts. As soon as he started the Adult Program, he immediately lost interest in Lego and became obsessed with the computer, writing lengthy stories about home construction. It was as if the manual activity of Lego had compensated for being forced to use his mind in school, while the mental activity of writing compensated for repetitious manual tasks in the workshop.

Far more challenging: John's behavior deteriorated, with escalating irritation and distress. Morgan Center responded with firmness and with attempts to enrich his program. We tried megadoses of B6 and magnesium, which had worked before, but this time seemed to make him more irritable. We were suddenly on the brink of losing the only placement suitable for him, but once again good fortune intervened—the Adult Program was split into two rooms, roughly by ability. The staff person in charge of John's room, Sue Taylor, returned from a year away. Sue was one of his favorites, and her absence had no doubt contributed to John's distress. Additional activity and variety in the smaller room kept his attention focused. We stopped B6 and started DMG at Dr. Rimland's suggestion; it had a noticeable calming effect.

Our close call taught me a lesson: while adults with autism may grow in their ability to cope with the outer world, they follow their own timetable. Many, like John, will always need support, and even in a familiar setting, the wrong mix of circumstances can be disruptive. Our experience underlines the importance of a variety of programs suitable for adult needs; one size does not fit all. And no matter how well things may be going, placement security can never be taken for granted.

A holding pattern

In 2001 Morgan Center moved to a new site some twenty miles away. Because of space limitations, all the adults were back in one room. For the first time, John rode a para-transit bus with several of his peers. We faced multiple changes with apprehension, but amazingly, the transition was almost entirely smooth.

John's longtime friend Sue Taylor now heads the Adult Program, and with her calm and skill, the daily schedules are carefully planned so that the adults are rarely all crammed into the same space at once. Workshop-like tasks are organized so that everyone can participate, regardless of ability. While language therapy is not funded for adults, the program makes a heroic effort to sustain language goals.

The downside is that it's difficult to retain capable staff with the meager reimbursement paid by the State, forcing a lifelong commitment to fundraising by those parents who are still on their feet, as well as requiring perpetual response to erosion of state support. For if the potential for adults to learn is there, the funding isn't; in most states, adults with autism receive less than one-third the program support funding of the earlier years, and even that is diminishing. *For me, the hardest part of our experience has not been John himself, but rather the difficulty of obtaining and keeping services.*

John's career has spanned three eras: from total lack of public support for special education as a child, to the empowerment of IDEA (1975), to the 2004 IDEA revision which undermined some parental rights. Similarly, California has evolved from meager services for special needs (pre-1970), to a no-frills statewide delivery system (1970s–1990s), to the economic backlash of the early 2000s, which has threatened to dismantle the whole structure. The unraveling of rights and services in California, in the name of "cost containment," has been exacerbated by the tremendous increase in the autism population. The result of these changes is that there's no assurance that an adult child will be cared for, once the parents are gone.

Our children grow up, and we grow old. My peers, who've coped with the issues of autism for so many years, seem to have an unduly high rate of mortality and illness for their age. Lifelong stress is surely a factor: parents must not only determine their affected child's needs and find (or fight for) adequate services, but also perform an elaborate juggling act to sustain the rest of the family. Those who are lucky find stable programs and adequate support. Even then, they face the perpetual task of keeping those services afloat.

Despite hard realities, living with autism is an immensely enriching experience. Autism can bring its own blessings in our personal growth, in our children's unique gifts, and in the incredible people dedicated to their care, people who wouldn't come into our lives any other way.

Special gifts

Back in 1972, my psychic consultant insisted that many autistic children possessed unusual gifts, in some cases surpassing the skills of normal children. (She said, "Give John a guitar. You'll be amazed what he does with it!" We gave John a small guitar for Christmas, and he promptly stepped on it and smashed it with a loud twang. She was right: I *was* amazed.) I was reminded of her comment in 1978, when *Psychology Today* published an article by Dr. Bernard Rimland, entitled "Inside the Mind of the Autistic Savant." I was fascinated to read that one in ten autistic children exhibited some form of special talent, while one in a hundred might possess a gift far beyond the ability of a normal person the same age. (It was all right to say "normal" in 1978, as opposed to today's politically correct "neurotypical" or "typically functioning.")

The article listed special abilities in declining order of frequency, including: music (perfect pitch, tonal memory, ability to reproduce complex songs at an early age); memory (memorizing TV credits, recall of events in infancy); art (ability to copy, faithful reproduction of detail); "pseudo-verbal" (ability to remember, spell, and pronounce words, usually without full comprehension); mathematics (fascination with numbers, knowing the answer without doing the problem); geographic (memorization of maps); coordination (ability to balance objects or climb to high places without fear); extrasensory perception (saying names others were thinking, knowing who was on the phone); multiple skills (more than one of the above).

Also in 1978, as if on cue, John sat down one day and drew a floor plan. The lines were wobbly, but everything was in place: windows, doors, appliances, fixtures. The only feature out of proportion was a huge closet. When I asked him whose house it was, he replied, "Kevin," and recited the address. I was stunned. Kevin's mother and I used to exchange babysitting in our old neighborhood, but John pointedly hadn't been invited back since he was two years old, in 1965. He hadn't set foot in that house for 13 years. His drawing was accurate except for the large closet, where I remembered Kevin had kept his toys. John always hid in the toy closet and refused to leave until I returned; it obviously loomed as large in his memory as in the drawing. Subsequently, we discovered that John had almost total recall of remodeling projects and new appliances back to the age of 18 months, a time when he'd seemed completely tuned out and unaware of his surroundings.

Following publication of the savant article, Dr. Rimland was scheduled to visit Morgan Center, and out of curiosity we conducted an informal survey of families to see if any of the students exhibited special abilities. To our surprise, they *all* did to one degree or another, though there was only one "prodigious savant," a boy who could recite calendar dates in past and future and never forgot the year anyone was born (to our peril, as we aged!). For his part, John was drawing more and more elaborate floor plans, including an entire terminal at San Francisco International Airport. He displayed unusual tonal memory (though far from perfect pitch), humming snatches of tunes as complex as the middle of a Bach fugue. He also would occasionally startle me by saying aloud the name of someone I was thinking about—always someone he knew. Sometimes I realized that I might have been talking about the person, but other times I definitely had not. Oddly, the "ESP" disappeared as John became more verbal, only recurring when his seizure medication needed adjusting.

As Dr. Rimland pointed out in his article, the special abilities of the autistic savant children were "largely those considered functions of the right hemisphere" (an oversimplification, he was quick to add). Looking at John and his peers with new eyes, I realized that all were deficient in the left-brained linear thinking on which we pride ourselves in Western culture; they couldn't reason as we did, and had trouble understanding our rules. If the left hemisphere was damaged or dysfunctional, did the right hemisphere overdevelop in compensation? And why did all the children at Morgan Center show evidence of unusual gifts? Was it because they'd received such intensive treatment, allowing their talents to manifest? John's drawings and interest in maps stemmed from the efforts of his teachers, but he never could have been taught at all without the right kind of intervention opening the door to begin with. He was one of the lucky ones; I wonder how many other children might have unique abilities hidden behind difficult behavior.

Whatever the case, the *Psychology Today* article and Dr. Rimland's visit fostered new appreciation of the unique attributes within autism. The article was followed by a flurry of network TV productions and newspaper features, with some of the Morgan Center students becoming fleeting celebrities. The downside was an increasing number of skeptics who felt that it was impossible for nonverbal children to be anything but retarded. Interestingly enough, all the children blossomed when special attention was given to their apparent gifts—and all withered when attention was withdrawn in a growing atmosphere of criticism. (The same phenomenon occurred during the Facilitated Communication controversy of the early 1990s. Without doubt, some children who don't speak can communicate intelligently by other means. Unfortunately, the hype surrounding FC and the sloppiness of some of its practitioners led to discrediting of the capabilities of all nonverbal children.)

In 1989 savants once again made headlines with release of the movie *Rain Man*, for which Dr. Rimland was technical advisor. The movie coincided with publication of a book called *Extraordinary People*, by Darold A. Treffert, MD. Dr. Treffert also assisted in the making of *Rain Man*, sharing his fascination for savants, autistic and otherwise. The movie and book did much to increase public awareness and appreciation of autism, at least for a while.

Special people

Morgan Center's Founder and Director, Louise Emerson, is one of the unsung pioneers in the field of autism. Before coming to California, she taught autistic children at a Yale University clinic with a ratio of 2:1, an approach that she said "almost worked." With great determination, she started her own experimental program in California in 1969, with four children, four teachers, and no funding. Even when John started Morgan Center in 1973, the teachers were still creating and Xeroxing their own teaching materials. In 1975, the passage of PL 94-142 gradually provided funding support, and by 1978, when the first autism classes in public schools were forced into law in California, the techniques of special education had become accepted practice. What made Morgan Center unique was Louise's uncanny ability as a diagnostician; she devoured research and possessed an inner radar for sizing up a child's strengths and weaknesses. Before her retirement in 2000, she'd trained several generations of teachers, including her longtime assistant Jennifer Sullivan, now Morgan Center's Executive Director. Today the program serves some 45 children and 30 adults, and remains a model for successful intervention.

Bernard Rimland was already a legend by the time I met him in 1975, as his landmark book *Infantile Autism* had largely discredited the damage done by Bruno Bettelheim's "Refrigerator Mother" theory of causation. We became better acquainted in 1989, when John and I made an impromptu visit to his office at the Autism Research Institute (ARI) in San Diego.

Visitors were greeted at a secretary's tidy desk, behind which loomed another, covered with a mountain of papers. With the aplomb of a magician whisking a tablecloth out from under the silverware, Dr. Rimland thrust his hand into the middle of the precarious pile and extracted one item without causing an avalanche, remarking casually that I might be interested to see what his son Mark was doing. It was a beautiful picture; Mark had become an accomplished artist. (I was later privileged to include Mark's artwork in a number of exhibits in California and at ASA national conferences.) This visit made me aware of what went on behind the scenes at ARI; in addition to his widely known research and writing, Dr. Rimland was an astonishingly generous one-man support group for families all over the world. Even in retirement, he remained the towering figure in the world of autism treatment and research, particularly in the cutting-edge field of biomedical research, as carried forth by DAN! (Defeat Autism Now!). His unwavering passion to conquer autism changed the lives of all families with children on the spectrum, past and future, whether they ever met him or not. His passing in 2006 leaves a void in the field, and in all our hearts.

Miriam Lee was not involved with autism at all, yet her impact on John was dramatic. A friend had recommended acupuncture for hyperactivity. An escapee from Mao's China, Miriam Lee was notorious in a good way, as the person responsible for legalizing acupuncture in California. Though her English and John's language were both limited, they communicated with absolute clarity, and she let him know who was boss. Initially, she treated John for hyperactivity and alertness: John, who was touch-sensitive, would protest mightily as the needles were inserted, then relax with a goofy grin for an hour or more, looking like a contented porcupine. Teachers noted his increased awareness, though unfortunately his schedule did not allow for enough continuing treatments to make a lasting difference. While Miriam has long since retired, John still demands acupuncture for sore throats, and always seems disappointed when conventional physicians don't *do* something to make him feel better.

These three remarkable people also represent the three strongest fields of influence in John's life: special education, advocacy, and alternative approaches to health and well-being.

Advocacy: a necessary evil

If autism was initially an isolating experience, the solution came in joining forces with other families who were in the same boat. In 1965 Dr. Rimland founded the National Society for Autistic Children (now Autism Society of America), and in 1973 a friend and I started a local chapter in our county. At that time, autism was still excluded from emerging services for the developmentally disabled; our focus was to ensure that our children would qualify for these services by being recognized as "disabled" rather than "disturbed," i.e. as having an inherent problem rather than one inflicted by their parents. By the late 1970s autistic children were not only receiving funding for support services but also were allowed to attend public schools (in separate classes, of course).

As often happens when families receive what they need, they become complacent. There followed a long period when autistic children were served (if not always with excellence) within the system as a matter of course, at least in California, and the intense activism waned. But this period of relative calm was shattered by a variety of changes that combined to make the lives of today's families at once more precarious—and more promising—than ever before:

- *The trend toward inclusion.* The political thrust toward full inclusion originated with advocacy for the physically disabled, culminating in ADA (the Americans with Disabilities Act of 1990, mandating full access to facilities). "Person-first" language transformed the phrase *disabled individuals* to *individuals with disabilities*, and *autistic children* to *children with autism*. Parents began to demand that their children be fully included in neighborhood schools, a still-evolving trend. My son's generation was the first in special education classes, and today's affected children are the first in regular classes, a setting not yet fully prepared to receive them.

- *New treatments.* Services and treatments were sparse during John's childhood, but at least the choices were simpler. Dr. Rimland demonstrated through the DAN! Conferences that autism *is* treatable biomedically, but today's parents must choose from a bewildering and growing array of additional interventions that may be helpful to some, but not to others. A spate of books by parents of "recovered" children has resulted in periodic stampedes toward new approaches, e.g. auditory integration training, facilitated communication, options therapy, behavior modification (now called Applied Behavior Analysis, or ABA). Many physicians are still ill-informed or skeptical, and parents are faced with a multitude of choices they must make on their own, complicated by the urgent feeling that precious time will be irretrievably lost without early intervention.

- *The autism epidemic.* The greatest threat is the autism explosion, not only overwhelming families and the entire services delivery system, but potentially threatening society and the economy as well. Like most other states, California is ill-equipped to deal with the onslaught. Today's parents must struggle as hard to retain services as the preceding generation struggled to obtain them in the first place. I am greatly impressed by the younger parents: intelligent, articulate, dedicated, far more knowledgeable than we were—and, I fear, wearing out as rapidly.

As a result of all these factors, grassroots advocacy is once again a driving force, with energetic new groups leaving older, more conservative organizations in their wake. It is an exciting time to have a child with autism because there is new hope, but in some ways it's also a far more difficult time than the previous two decades. After some twenty years of a pleasant lack of involvement with political activism, I now find it necessary to work as hard as I did in the 1970s to try to protect John's current programs. And it's discouraging that some of my cohorts of the past three decades are expiring before their time.

Growing up with segregation

I have sometimes wondered what would have become of John if he'd been born in a different era. If he were older, he'd probably have joined the 95 percent in institutions, drugged and barely manageable, misdiagnosed as psychotic or, in his adult years, as retarded. One hears very little about senior citizens with autism, and except for a lucky few who may have managed to live with their eccentricities, they are a population lost to us, as we are to them.

John's age group is transitional; their shortcomings reflect the lack of appropriate services until late childhood or adolescence. Yet he and his peers should inspire younger families, for many of these adult children now lead happy, productive lives. Some have jobs, and many have revealed late-onset talents, especially in the field of art. They remind us all that it's never too late for gains to occur (a view, alas, not shared by most funding agencies).

If John had been born today, his diagnosis and treatment would come earlier, but unless early intervention or biomedical treatment were miraculously successful in his case, I suspect that a good share of his autism would remain. I'm not sure I would insist upon an inclusive setting for him in today's climate; John is too aware of his surroundings to be comfortable where he's not wanted.

Full inclusion in public schools is still in its pioneering phase. At best, it's an enriching experience for all concerned, and while I greatly admire the heroic families who have made it work, I fear that in some cases the crusade itself may take precedence over the child's best interests. I also suspect that some who push so hard for inclusion have their hearts set on their child becoming "normal," an understandable goal, but one which may not be possible except in a few cases. Stories like Catherine Maurice's *Let Me Hear Your Voice*, while inspiring, have prompted unrealistic expectations. If our children teach us any lessons, it's that each is unique, and what works best for one may not succeed with the next. Much work needs to be done in educating the public and in providing adequate funding before full inclusion will become commonplace and reliable, if ever.

John is probably in the best place he could be at this point in his life. His program of some thirty years has evolved to meet his needs, and he's benefited greatly from the continuity that's sorely lacking in the public sector. While his program is highly respected, specialized schools are unpopular with the education establishment and are regarded by many younger parents as "segregated" or "medieval." Adult programs in which all clients come together (site-based) are gradually being replaced by those in which clients wander (community-based), providing fiscal economy in the name of inclusiveness.

Is it so dreadful that John has grown up with other children like himself? Even in a somewhat protected setting, he's achieved many of the goals of inclusion. He's at home in our community and is welcomed by name in stores and restaurants (never mind that he rearranges the produce or draws floor plans on paper placemats). He has a comfortable group of peers with similar needs, and genuine friends among the staff. During his adult years, he's become far more sociable and adaptable to change. He's learned a variety of work skills (and ways to vary them, including the art of sealing envelopes under the table with his knee). He's worn out three computers writing wishful stories about neighborhood remodeling projects and proposed trips. He's the greatest living fan of United Airlines Mileage Plus, even when flights are delayed and luggage lost, and he displays whimsical good humor—most of the time.

As for us, my husband and I have been especially fortunate in finding skilled program staff for respite (paid privately, I might add, since little public support for respite is available), enabling us to have a taste of "normal" life, which we appreciate all the more as a rare treat. For her part, our daughter has survived the trials of growing up with autism to become a wise and mature person with a family of her own. We've all been extremely lucky.

Conclusion: survival

John's remaining deficits are part of his autism, and I doubt they would have been remedied in any setting. He's baffled in unfamiliar places and can't be trusted to *always* look before crossing the street, like the stereotype of the absent-minded professor. Communication skills are limited. Money holds no significance for him, though it does for us: funding for services is perpetually uncertain, as is John's future. We'd like him to remain in his program and live in a family setting when we're no longer around, but there are no guarantees.

On a good day, the bus is on time and John is eager to leave, and he looks forward to spending the night with a staff member whom he enjoys, and I look forward to sleeping late the following morning. On a not-so-good day, a new bus driver is lost because the regular bus company went out of business due to budget cuts, John informs me that "poor sick John" wants to stay home (but he is chuckling, and I don't let him), and I receive a dozen new e-mails about proposed elimination of services. On a really bad day, we are all genuinely sick, including poor John, and I receive 47 "URGENT!" e-mails, and every member of our parent group is in crisis, and I don't think I'll live through it.

But the good days far outnumber the bad, and I can only conclude with yet another far-seeing pronouncement from the psychic, so long ago: "You must demonstrate," she said, "that it is worth the effort to nurture these special children." And she was right. It is.

TWENTY-TWO

Edith P. Gray

When our son was nearly 15, we took him to Vienna for a consultation with Professor Hoff, a professor of psychiatry and neurology, who introduced us to a psychologist for a variety of tests.

Michael had little experience with sports of any kind, and in Vienna they enrolled him in a gymnastics program. The first day he ventured only three steps up the ladder, but by the end of the week he could climb to the top of one ladder that reached the ceiling, move over to an adjacent ladder, and come down. I could see that he could meet new challenges, and that he was very proud of himself.

When the four weeks were over, Professor Hoff gave us a letter saying, "Though Michael is retarded, there still seems to be a lot of room for improvement." He wanted us to send Michael to Los Angeles to work with a former student of his. I've always regretted that I didn't follow through, but the cost of $500 per month was a lot of money then, and I was always appeasing my husband Leon, and that's why Michael didn't go there.

Before going to Vienna, I'd been made to feel there was something wrong with me. I didn't trust my judgment any more, and so I asked Professor Hoff, who'd observed me over the four weeks, if I could see him on my own behalf, telling him how I felt.

"No," he said, "You go back, keep away from psychologists and therapists, and use your own good common sense." It felt good to get his reassurance—it made all the difference in my feelings about myself.

Professor Hoff also saw my other son, Anthony, and tested his IQ, which proved to be 168—and the test was in German! Anthony was a great help to me at that time. There is no doubt that the siblings of a retarded child suffer. Although I tried to back Anthony up on many occasions, he still was at a disadvantage. How could it be otherwise?

I used to tell him, "You share in our blessings. You have to share in our sorrows too." He did. In some way he benefited: he matured at an early age, and has played a big role in our family. He still does. He's a successful man and a wonderful husband and father.

Meanwhile, the psychologist in Vienna told me she'd made up her mind about me and wanted me to take a Rorschach test to confirm her impressions. She said that the test revealed I was a very practical person, and that I tied it all up with a beautiful bow—very feminine!

We became good friends. One day I went to her when it seemed my best recourse was to commit suicide and take Michael with me. She agreed that my situation was very bad indeed, and she could see why I felt the way I did. Having said that, she expressed confidence that I would find a way out. She was right. In some situations we need a truly good and understanding friend who believes in us.

So the boys and I went on our way feeling much better about ourselves. Anthony drove us through the beautiful Austrian countryside. We saw a hotel and we turned in. Dinnertime had passed, but they received us with open arms and before we knew it, there was a wonderful meal before us. They couldn't keep us for the night, but they called a neighbor who put us up and accepted no money from us. I always was amazed at how normal Michael acted in a normal environment: he behaved beautifully!

We got to France. We were worried about the directions to Paris, so we pulled into a service station right behind a French couple. I asked the driver for directions and he said, "Follow me." We had a good guide, and followed him for many miles. We saw a bit of that beautiful city passing through on our way to England.

While in England, we witnessed something that I've told parents of handicapped children about, particularly those who were advised by doctors to abandon their babies…to leave them at the hospital and not even take them home. My cousin and her husband absolutely adored cats.

One day a strange cat came into the living room with a kitten in her mouth, placed it before the fireplace, licked it all over, and left. The mother cat looked rather the worse for wear. Next day she came again, licked the kitten again, played with it a bit, and left. And the next day, my cousin found the mother cat dead in the garden. She'd placed her offspring in what seemed to her to be a good home, so that she could die in peace knowing her baby was with good people.

Of course I thought of Michael, and when my time comes to die, will I find a place for him so that I can go in peace?

Adapted from Edith Gray's book *What Michael Taught Me*, © 1994.

TWENTY-THREE

Beth Sposato

My name is Beth, and I'm a landlady. At no time in my younger life did I ever wish to be that, but my son John has autism, and while searching for a place for him to live in 1996, I made the sudden decision to become his landlady because *I* would never evict him, and I could keep his rent low. The arrangement has worked well, and now, ten years later, our experience might be useful to anyone considering a similar step.

John was born in 1965. It was obvious by the time he was three that something was amiss. (I'm omitting here the long-running saga of his school career.) Because there was no other placement available for him, and because he had to be someplace, circumstances led to the state mental hospital. (In Nebraska they're called Regional Centers.) More than a dozen of his adult years were spent there.

In early 1996 (John was 31) the state informed us that he could be served in the community, and we chose one of the local service providers. They would have the task of hiring and training staff for the residence, and I began to look at houses and apartments that were advertised for rent in the newspaper. My intention was to save the agency some of the legwork involved in finding a suitable apartment or house, but as I toured the available rentals, the thought came to me that I could just buy one, and be his landlady. If nothing else, I could avoid the awkward, probably necessary explanation of why my son, in his thirties, was not out searching for a place himself.

I found a house that seemed right. It was within walking distance of banks and bus stops and a few stores, and that seemed better than isolating John in outer suburbia. Because it was on a corner lot with extended length behind it, only one other house was actually close. The floor plan provided a bedroom that was suitable for overnight staff. A downstairs suite of rooms in the walkout lower floor was suitable for a housemate, while also giving that person some privacy; the first floor of the house and the downstairs suite (with its own full bathroom) connect through the laundry room.

I elected not to tell the neighbors anything. Explaining that John was in the state's most secure mental hospital because of autism (which I consider to be a brain disorder, not a psychiatric disorder) would have been unnecessarily complicated. His primary diagnosis was autism, and he could score in the normal range on an IQ test, so he wasn't eligible for services within the 1996 mental retardation system. People who were not personally impacted by that issue were unaware of problems within the system, problems that resulted in his placement in the Regional Center. Legislative changes a few years before had introduced the term "developmental disability" to replace mental retardation as the criteria for eligibility in its non-institutional system, but there were issues—like a long waiting list—still to be resolved.

If the house were to be occupied by, say, an elderly relative who chose to have an on-the-premises personal assistant to help with a variety of tasks related to daily living, there could be no objection to that. Why should a parallel situation involving a young adult with autism have to be run past the neighbors in advance of the house purchase?

I had already concluded that he was in no way a danger to the neighborhood. If I thought he was, I would have opposed community placement.

John moved in on the Labor Day weekend in 1996. Because he was new to the agency which had accepted him, he was double-staffed for the opening weeks—that is, two fulltime up-and-awake staff 24 hours a day. Because things went well, that arrangement was very soon reduced to having one person there whenever he was home.

The family of the first young man who stayed in the downstairs rooms was disenchanted with the service provider after a few months, so they found another service provider and moved their son out. The tenant who came to replace him is a good one and a pleasant companion for John. He and my son have become friends, and enjoy doing many things together. One staff person in the house supervises both men. During the day they both are out of the house, overseen by a separate agency that handles vocational services and provides job coaches. In some years, day activities have included part-time paid work; at other times just volunteer work.

Buying the house was almost an impulse decision. I didn't do much research on what might be involved. My husband agreed to the undertaking, and helped with the bank loans, but mostly I'm the one who deals with the details involved in ownership.

For IRS purposes, the house is treated as income property and handled accordingly on our tax return. Our wills specify that when we're both gone a trust will be created with John's share of our estate, and the house will become a part of the trust. (An alternate way would be to leave it to a foundation created a few years ago by some parents, for the purpose of owning property leased to the service-providing agency.)

Here is how the financial aspects of the ownership are handled: the two men who live there pay rent to me. I deposit their rent checks in a bank account set up just for this house. From that account I write checks to pay the mortgage, the gas bill, electricity, the water bill, and for home repairs. The tenants pay for trash removal and they buy their own groceries (staff assist with this, of course).

Because his income is low, my son qualified for a rent subsidy from the local Housing Authority. That subsidy is paid directly to me, the landlady. The Housing Authority deposits a monthly subsidy into the house's checking account. A few years after John was approved for the subsidy, the Housing Authority wrote some new rules, and one of them forbade paying subsidies if the property owner and the tenant were in the same family. We were granted a waiver, but it's likely that anyone trying to create a similar arrangement now wouldn't be approved, at least where we live.

The salaries of the staff people who work at the house are paid by the agency that serves John and the other tenant. The source of the agency's budget is a blend of federal and state dollars. We're fortunate to have chosen an agency that was flexible enough to allow our housing arrangement. (The more typical arrangement for the agency is to lease a home and buy the groceries for the people they serve, and then bill them for room and board.)

John has income through the Social Security Administration, part of it in the form of SSI and part of it disability income (SSDI). When he has a paying job, the SSI is reduced.

Those are the details of what works for us. Now for the downside: we lose money every month. (Since John is our son, we are of course willing to do this.) When we first took the plunge, it was my hope that the rent we collected would cover the mortgage payment. It doesn't. Every month I must deposit personal funds into the bank account for that house. Even with the Housing Authority subsidy, the rent collected doesn't quite equal the mortgage payment. Raising the rent is not a simple option. It would involve getting the permission of the Housing Authority during the few weeks that precede their contract renewal each year. Moreover, they have a ceiling on the amount of rent a subsidized tenant can be charged. (In other words, the Housing Authority won't subsidize anything fancy, because subsidies are for people who really need help.)

The Housing Authority requires a once-a-year inspection of rental units that it subsidizes, and is rather strict about maintenance, smoke detectors, etc.; the property must pass inspection before a rent contract is renewed. The Housing Authority also has strict rules about who may be a part of a household that it subsidizes. These regulations, of course, are safeguards both for tenants and for the public's money. We could reject the subsidy and not have to deal with the regulations, but without the subsidy John would be paying the full amount of his monthly rent, and that would leave him with less money for other things.

A second reason that house outgo exceeds income is that every few months something needs repair. Since buying the house, we've had to replace the water heater and the furnace, and that was after a couple of seasons of frequent furnace repair bills. Plumbing leaks on the main floor sent water into a closet several times, and by the time that problem was solved the repairs had totaled more than $1000. Rainwater coming into the basement was another problem that had to be dealt with. Faucet repairs, still another. I've had to buy a new storm door, make electrical repairs, and repair the garage door after it was mysteriously damaged. The roof was replaced a year ago. Neither John nor his house-mate are destructive. If they were, that would be an additional cost.

A separate, potential source of problems is the neighborhood. When the house was purchased we had no idea that the service provider we'd chosen was already operating a mini group home across the street and down a few doors. At least one neighbor complained to the city about there being two group homes in one area. That problem was resolved with a letter explaining that John's house was privately owned and he would be receiving assistance and support there but it could not be called a "group home." A few years later the other residence, which had been home to some women with developmental disabilities, was changed back to a home for a regular family.

I sometimes feel as though some of the neighbors are watching for something to criticize. I would prefer a supportive attitude, with neighbors volunteering to keep an eye on things for the sake of the residents, and maybe even welcoming these two developmentally disabled men as part of the community. Maybe someday.

A few years ago the staff did organize an Open House and on another occasion an outdoor barbeque for people living up and down the street. Lots of people came, and I'm sure that some of John's neighbors are nice people who don't mind his presence on their block.

At a time in life when my husband and I should naturally be having fewer responsibilities, we seem to have added more. I hope that the picture I've sketched here will help you decide if you want to attempt a similar housing arrangement or not. As the property owner, you may gain a degree of leverage or control over what happens to your offspring with disabilities, but you will also probably have some additional hassles.

I've heard of variations on this house-owning theme. For example, own a duplex and have a non-handicapped tenant occupy one half in exchange for certain services for the residents of the other half. Or have the person with the disability own his or her own house. More about this option is available from a group called Home of Your Own and they have a website which can be accessed with the keyword, HOYO.

For several years my son referred to his residence as "John and Bob's new home." Recently he has adopted another name. He calls it his "PLF" which he says is an abbreviation for "permanent living facility." The term amuses me. I don't know who suggested it. But he seems happy in his PLF, since he's never asked me when he's going to be discharged.

John's wake

I don't mean the kind of wake that's a pre-funeral gathering; rather, I'm thinking about the widening path that a boat leaves behind it on the surface of the water.

From age seven to nine, John was served by the Judevine Center in suburban St. Louis, Missouri. Near the end of his two years there, he was placed in a regular classroom experimentally, so that the teachers who worked with him at the Center could observe his behavior and devise remedies for any problems. Even though this placement was experimental and temporary, some of the students in the cooperating school became interested in autism because of him, and did some fund-raising for the cause.

In another school, after we'd moved to another state, the woman who taught one of my other children volunteered to help in a fundraising project of the local chapter of the Autism Society. Even after we left the area, she continued to volunteer for the autism cause.

When John was of high school age, I hired a young man to work with him to supplement what John's school was able to provide. After only a short time, he noticed that even with John's social and behavioral handicaps, he was capable in algebra; that young man decided to return to school and finish his own education. He said, "If John can do it, so can I."

The wake that John leaves is observable in my own life. First, it made me more humble. As time went by, other benefits emerged; I attended conferences in places I'd never visited; I met new people; as volunteer editor of the ASA national newsletter, I got pretty good with word-processing and computers—something that might not have occurred without that motivation, and that's been a good thing. In short, my life has changed in many good ways.

The most fun event in the wake of John's autism came when the educational program that he was part of decided that he could be given a high school diploma. We decided that a small private ceremony was in order. One of the teachers loaned a cap and gown. A local radio station made me a tape of *Pomp and Circumstance* so we could have "graduation music," and in front of some assembled classmates, guests and family members, he was given his diploma. The fun part for me was that I appointed myself the commencement speaker, a privilege I know I would never have under any other circumstances!

I've met many parents for whom their child's autism was a catalyst for their own really significant achievements; some have run for public office, others made dramatic career changes, started schools, founded service agencies, were propelled into research, launched foundations, published books, developed curricula, began special programs and camps, not to mention serving within, testifying to, and reforming whole public systems. In step with them have been an army of professionals who've joined the cause and made their own valuable contributions. We call it autism, but it's also a boatload of opportunity with its own ever-widening wake that creates waves big enough to rock lives and change the course of social institutions.

Drug treatments

When John was in his early teens the moment came when we chose to try medication as a way to deal with the awful collection of behaviors confronting us. (I can't recreate here what those years were like—imagine needing to keep your younger children safe from an older brother who might throw furniture.) We'd regarded drugs as the wrong approach to behavior problems, but when things got bad, we began to think of them as a possibly useful tool. We first tried Haldol. Within days his arms locked into pretzel-like positions ("extra-pyramidal effects"), making it impossible for him to have functional use of his hands for hours at a time.

As the drug regimen continued, other experiences emerged. (By now I've forgotten exactly what was prescribed for him, mostly on a try-it-and-see basis. I do know there was an extended time on Thorazine.) He was drowsy a lot of the time, often lying in his bed in a lightly unconscious state. It certainly made him easier to deal with and the household calmer, but he spent so much time napping that on some days I felt as if I were keeping a dead body in his room. It didn't seem right to me. It bothered me that he could no longer do even simple arithmetic, and in the past one of the pleasures in his life had been working out answers to complicated algebra problems. Then I noticed that his handwriting (really more like printing than writing) had become impossible to read.

Other things about the use of medication bothered me. One, a lot of the motive for using it was to make me feel more secure, and not necessarily to benefit my son. Two, in order to deal with behavior that occurred only a small percentage of the time, he had to take pills which would subdue him

to some degree 24 hours a day. There was no drug that could be administered at the moment of an outburst, but I wished there were. One psychiatrist dubbed my wish the "Marlin Perkins School of Medicine" when I
spoke of needing a drug like those tranquilizer darts that could stop an
animal in its tracks on *Wild Kingdom* on TV. I couldn't imagine politely
asking my son in the middle of a violent eruption, "Here, would you take
this pill." Once an outburst is in progress, there is no reasoning with that
person, so medication has to begin ahead of time, and be in effect all the
time.

Around this time (four or five years since the first attempt to medicate
him) he left home and was admitted to a psychiatric hospital, due to
increasing problems in school. He went to one other place, and finally was
placed in the state mental hospital a few miles from our home. He was 18.

During the years in the state hospital there were stretches of time with
no psychotherapeutic medication at all. Also during those years, we saw the
disturbing symptoms of tardive dyskinesia (involuntary muscle movements). A lot of his aggressive behavior seemed to be caused by divergence
from the "script" that seemed to dominate his brain. I don't know if an
Obsessive Compulsive Disorder drug was ever tried, but something else
did make a dramatic difference.

I visited him in the hospital on weekends, and on Wednesdays I would
take him out for a home visit. Usually I let him choose where we would go
on those days, and often he chose the grocery store—always a source of
tension for me because I couldn't buy him everything he wanted, but
neither did I want to risk the eruption of a public spectacle when I turned
him down. Nevertheless, the Wednesday trip to the grocery store became a
weekly routine for us for several years.

On one such trip I realized that he seemed unusually agreeable to
whatever purchase decisions I made. My "yes" or "no" didn't seem to matter.
Then I realized that this had been the case for two or three weeks in succes-
sion. My fears about an episode of disruptive behavior in the grocery store
faded. His occasional odd and unexpected (and usually too loud) speech
remained. The repetitive, characteristic, and seemingly irrelevant questions
that were typical for him remained, but the scary glitter in his eyes had disappeared and his rigid adherence to routine had softened. I was relieved
and relaxed. And pleased. Going to the store became a far more pleasant
routine than it had been. I knew that something was clearly different and I
had a hunch about what it was, so I called his caseworker at the hospital and

asked him to check if a new medication had been started. The answer was yes. The medication was Prozac.

In subsequent months his medication was changed again, and the improvement continued. He began taking Luvox (fluvoxamine). He remains on it today and I credit the Luvox for greatly improving my son's quality of life. His language has become more conversational. His rocking has almost entirely disappeared. He rarely bites himself in frustration. At age 41 he's been taking Luvox for over a dozen years, and he is far more pleasant to be around than ever before in his adult life. It took over a decade of tinkering to find a helpful drug. The one that finally made a difference didn't exist when we first decided to try medication. He also takes general medical drugs such as a multi-vitamin and a decongestant, and two that are related to behavior issues, in addition to the Luvox. They are chlorpromazine and lorazepam, both for anxiety control. Our state's service-providing system mandates drug reviews at regular intervals to determine if a person needs to continue on prescribed drugs.

As a child, John was average-sized. Now, as a 41-year-old man, he is rather heavy. I believe that some, maybe all, of the extra weight that he's put on is related to drug therapy. He's always been interested in food and would probably eat non-stop if those of us around him didn't tell him to quit. My husband and I have become heavy as we've aged, so John's weight could be a combination of genetics plus the drug treatment. Over the last two decades we saw his weight increase and then decrease—once even to the point of gauntness—as different drug treatments were tried and abandoned.

In 1996 John was 31. It had been 12 years since he was admitted to the state hospital, and due to some internal machinations in the public institutions system that I can only guess at, he was chosen for placement in the community. The placement has been very successful.

Nacre

The oyster forms layers of nacre over an irritant such as a grain of sand, eventually changing the bit of alien matter into a smooth, iridescent sphere, beautiful and valued. The term "pearls of wisdom" is an apt expression for the insight gained in response to the unexpected stimulus that autism can be in a parent's life. Several people gave me pearls of wisdom that were immensely helpful along the way. Some things I figured out for myself. Here are a dozen of those pearls:

- Behavior Modification (or Applied Behavior Analysis—ABA—as it's now called) is best regarded as a useful tool rather than a lifestyle.

- Lois Blackwell of the Judevine Center offered the following question as a test for whether or not the place where a person lives is really home. "If you leave, do they move someone else into your room?"

- Mary Pape, who once labored in the autism "trenches" in Omaha, suggested this question as a concrete focus for the way you envision your child's future: "Who will invite your child for Christmas dinner after you're gone?"

- If you find yourself getting swamped by details, swept up with an ideology, or stalled by trivial choices, one way to get the perspective you need is with the Pine Box Test proposed by a friend of mine. I apply the test myself with this question: "Is this going to make any difference when someone is shoveling dirt onto the lid of my coffin?"

- Writing an IEP (Individualized Education Program) or Individual Program Plan is a lot easier than making it really work. It's kind of like the difference between sitting in a warm, dry classroom for a course in agriculture and pulling on your boots seven mornings a week and slogging out for another day of farm chores.

- When we first took steps to enroll our seven-year-old son in a program based on behavioral law, a program that proposed to help him by teaching him new behavior, some people we spoke with were aghast. Their belief was that there was something deeply wrong within the child—they were thinking of autism as an *emotional* problem within his psyche and not as the *brain* disorder that it is—and they believed covering over that alleged deep, unexpressed emotional problem with conditioned behavior, rather than resolving it with psychotherapy, would be an awful mistake. Their belief caused a dilemma for me and introduced serious doubt about whether or not we'd made the right choice in going for the behavioral program. Then one of my other kids asked me, "Are people naked when they have their clothes on?" After reflecting on a suitable answer to that question, I answered, "Well, yes they are. They are naked underneath their clothes." That question helped me to see that using behavior analysis to teach my son to act differently wasn't just covering up what was wrong. He was what he was. The principles of applied behavior analysis would make him become actually different. New behavior is not just a false front or a costume disguising one's nakedness. It causes a genuine change in a brain, a "rewiring" that gives the brain and the mind powers they didn't have before.

- Language and new behavior learned in response to creative conditioning (or ABA if you want to call it that) is to normal behavior what limping is to walking. It may not have the smooth and natural quality of language or behavior acquired in normal development, but it's certainly better than no language or behavioral skill at all.

- Prioritizing. As parents, we seem destined to work toward some ideal that's always out there on the horizon. The child we care about should someday have a better educational program, someday have a job, someday live independently, or someday fulfill yet another ideal that somebody is promoting. I realized years ago that if the day of reckoning were today—that is, if *my* life were over *or* my son were taken from this world—my regrets would not be focused on whether or not he had a competitive, paying job. Nor would it matter how much independence he'd achieved. The thing I would regret would be if he hadn't experienced joy in this world. Did he have the chance to swim or play in water just for the pleasure of it? Did he have the thrill of an amusement park ride? Did he get to do things that were fun for him? If you have a child with autism, don't be so goal-oriented that you choke off the chance for your child to have some pleasure in life.

- Another mother told how when the extent of her son's disabilities became known, her father counseled her that the boy would always have to be "number one" in everything she did for her family. That grandfather meant well, of course, but the mother realized that if her son were always in first place, then her daughters would always be in second place. And that, she knew, was just plain unfair.

- My son moved from childhood to adulthood during the tug-of-war between institutions and community-based programs. Although our state pioneered community-based programs, when things became desperate for us the only real option we had was an institution. I learned several things from the years he spent in one while we waited for something more appropriate to emerge:

    o   Institutions today are not the bleak and deprived settings that might have existed forty or more years ago. (Federal programs like Medicaid are probably partly responsible for this improvement.)

    o   People should take care to distinguish between *place* of care and *type* of care. People who advocate for institutions aren't advocating for neglect and mistreatment, which can occur in any setting, including a family home or a community-based residence. The people who work in institutions care about the persons they serve.

    o   Beware of any ideologist who frames your options as an either-or choice, and one choice as thoroughly bad. Sometimes there are third or fourth options and sometimes, even when the options are limited, one is not so bad.

    o   Given the chaos that a teen with autism can cause within a family, it may have been an act of kindness to both John and his siblings to have him live elsewhere. He was given a more structured environment. The other children in the family were permitted, by their brother's absence, to have a more normal home life.

- During our son's early and middle childhood, my husband and I held the opinion that medication was the wrong approach to solving problems with behavior. As our child grew larger and more aggressive, we came to understand that medication is a right and proper tool.

- What you choose should be solely for the benefit of your child, and not to prove someone's favorite theory. Be wary about doing something just to please the promoter of some ideology.

TWENTY-FOUR

Sharon Lettick Crotzer

My autistic brother is now 51 years old. Ben is the youngest of four children, and has influenced all of our lives. He was diagnosed as classically autistic and still doesn't talk. As a young child his behavior demanded constant attention, and as an adult he still needs overseeing. Yet Ben is a lucky guy, because he happened to be born to a mother who felt her son should live with dignity and in a manner that matched her high standards. My mother Amy Lettick became a frontrunner in the growing field of autism, eventually earning an honorary doctorate from Yale University for her work. She founded a safe place for her son and those like him to thrive in. Benhaven has helped and guided hundreds of Bens, and is celebrating its fortieth anniversary this year (2007).

Ben is also lucky because he's more classically autistic than some. This means he isn't unhappy about being "different." He has no ego problems, no financial woes, no relationship concerns. His life is not stressful, so he looks fifteen years younger than his age. In one of the quarterly reports that we siblings receive as his guardians, the staff wrote, "Ben is happy 97 percent of the time." I wonder who's counting those smiles, but I get the point. He's a lucky guy.

By learning sign language to communicate, his life has become less frustrating, and he's both more expressive and more understanding. He's held a job for many years where his unique dexterity is put to use, and he's appreciated and respected. He helps maintain his home by doing the grocery shopping, laundry, and vacuuming. He goes on vacations to the mountains and to the shore. His life is full and productive.

Ben didn't spontaneously acquire the skills that enable him to enjoy the life he leads today. Countless hours were spent breaking selected tasks into learnable routines, and this is still a continuing process. In his youth, he was cute and interestingly odd. But as puberty hit, he began to test his boundaries in his own way, eventually forcing my mother to create the live-in facility at Benhaven. A severely autistic adult is no longer cute and interesting, but potentially scary. He or she is physically stronger, and can be unpredictable. He can act inappropriately, unaware of danger. Parents need to honestly assess how this behavior affects not only their autistic child, but also the rest of the family.

Finding an acceptable living arrangement isn't easy, since there are still so few options. Benhaven remains one of the leading residential/educational facilities. It's now limited to Connecticut residents because of the extreme pressure of growing incidence, but it can be considered a model of what is possible.

If there is no residential facility near you, then help create one! Visit Benhaven and other residences to see how an autistic adult can continue to grow and learn and have enjoyable new experiences. But don't wait until the home situation is too stressful; plan ahead, and begin working for the future while it's still acceptable to have your child at home. This will provide the time needed to find a really good place, one that doesn't make parents feel as if they are giving up. Instead of feeling that they failed by not being able to maintain a life at home for their autistic child, parents need to think of the future in a positive way. A residence that caters to special needs, that offers activities and trips and experiences while also providing continued education, should not be considered a desperate last resort. Instead, parents should seek it out with the knowledge that life will improve for their child if they're exposed to things their parents can't provide.

As Ben aged, my mother tried her best to accept our reactions, and not be overwhelmed by his demands. I think one of the gifts that a parent can give the sibling of an autistic child is to openly discuss their jealousy for parental attention, their discomfort at appearing with him in public, and the fear of being hurt or embarrassed by the reactions of others. Although a parent hopes their neurotypical children won't have these emotions, these feelings need to be aired and allowed. It's difficult enough being a teenager without this extra burden. On the other hand, these lessons mold us into the adults we become. They teach us about humanity, and tolerance, and patience. Everyone is affected by his or her family growing up; having an autistic sibling makes the situation much more complex. As adults, we find our own paths and develop our particular coping skills. Some people find being part of a family with an autistic child inspiring, while others find it painful. Parents need to accept all reactions.

One of the areas in which my mother was a frontrunner was in defining some of the skills of Ben and others, and determining how they could be useful. For example, she paired two people who'd been considered rather "empty." She noted that one was dexterous but had an extremely short attention span, while the other, although unskilled in physical movements, was attentive. She teamed them up, and the skilled man was given a factory-type job putting parts together while the attentive one was taught to tap him on the shoulder to remind him to keep working. They both thrived, doing what was natural to each—they were productive.

Another area in which she was innovative was social skills. She felt that for Ben to be able to have enriching social experiences, he would need to learn the basics—how to eat properly, hold a fork, keep his napkin in his lap, wave hello to people, wait in line, etc. These skills would allow him to go out in public and join his family for dinner. She also helped him overcome his food fetishes. Working with Ben's pediatrician, my mother spent several miserable days while her son refused to eat the food served to everyone else. The doctor told her that eventually he would eat; Ben was stubborn and lasted many days, but I'll never forget watching him eat his first Chinese meal! Since then, he's become a good cook, enjoys an enormous variety of foods, and has had wonderful dining-out experiences with family, staff, and friends.

Ben used to have many self-stimulating routines ("stimming"). He would bang his hand on his ear, rock his head, wiggle his fingers in front of his face, and so on. With time and terrific guidance from staff, he's learned to stop doing these things in public. He's allowed to do them in the privacy of his own home or bedroom, but he's been taught what isn't socially acceptable. Additionally, his need for self-stimulation is relieved by exercise; he belongs to the YMCA, uses a treadmill or exercise bike at his house, hikes, rock climbs, and swims. As it does for the rest of us, aerobic exercise makes him feel good, and he smiles throughout his workouts. He's extremely fit as a result.

Being the parent to an autistic child isn't easy, and learning to handle the challenges is often painfully difficult. Not all lives are "happily ever after" ones, with or without autism. As the child approaches adulthood, more hurdles arise, demanding innovative action. Facing the realities of your child's autism doesn't have to be painful; it's all in how you look at it, and how creative you can be, given the situation.

TWENTY-FIVE

Ruth C. Sullivan

Many parents have written movingly about their children with autism and other developmental disabilities; the ups and downs, and the joys of reaching milestones, often the result of long and heroic effort. But there's almost nothing in print about the profound emotional impact on parents of placing their child outside the family home. (Because there isn't a pronoun in the English language to represent "his/her," I'll use "he/him" in what follows, for simplicity's sake.)

When these children move out, their 24-hour day is filled with strangers, often on 8-hour shifts, so their care now depends on many individuals. The parents become "visitors"; they worry that staff won't know or care enough about what makes him happy. Will the staff know when his feet are cold at night? Who will touch him affectionately? Will they make sure he looks nice? How long will it be before he considers the new place "home"? Will he be angry with his parents for "putting him away"? Will he understand why he needed to leave home? Will he think he's been abandoned, or that his family doesn't love him anymore? How do parents cope with the grief and the emptiness at home?

Professionals rarely recognize, much less address, the parents' feelings. In fact, in recent years I've been surprised to discover that even highly sensitive, experienced, caring staff haven't thought about the true depth of sadness and pain that most parents experience when placing their child in a residential setting. The ones I've spoken to simply assumed parents are filled with relief and happiness, especially when they believe that the agency operating the program is one they can trust.

Parents of children with severe language problems feel special concern, knowing it could be difficult or impossible for their child to report sadness, anxieties, unhappiness, or mistreatment; he might easily be misunderstood, and therefore extremely vulnerable to abuse. Adults with autism can be very strong and sometimes aggressive when agitated; parents may fear inexperienced staff will be impatient and punitive if not well-trained, monitored, and supported by knowledgeable and dedicated supervisors.

Whatever shred of hope there was for a child's normal life at home or on his own is now gone. The move requires a new image of one's grown child. He is now officially dependent, and probably always will be. Inexorably, he's joined the world of severely disabled adults.

Judy Barron, who in 1992 co-authored *There's a Boy in Here* with her son Sean, describes his leaving at age ten to live at a facility for emotionally disturbed children:

> When the day came to take him, I couldn't go. We packed his things in his new suitcase, bought him a little bright red rug to cheer up his room, filled his yellow footlocker—an attempt to hold off heartbreak with primary colors—and he and Ron got into the car… We hugged him good-bye… We waved until the car disappeared. Megan and I stood silently for a few minutes before she went to her room and closed the door. I lay down on the couch. I had never felt such loss. (p.134)

> The day was endless. Finally, Ron came home, his eyes red, his face ashen. Wordlessly we held each other for a long time. At last Ron said, "When I left him he seemed okay—I don't think he noticed." (p.135)

> I lay awake most of the night. Images flocked through my mind of Sean lying alone in that strange bed, abandoned, surrounded by strangers. He would be cold, I knew, because he always kicked off his covers, and we always went in and covered him. I wanted to cry, but there were no tears. (pp.135–6)

In *Mixed Blessings* (William and Barbara Christopher, 1989), Barbara Christopher and her housekeeper prepare Ned (age ten) for his move away from home. She wrote:

It was not the cheerful preparation that had gone into John's [their other son] departures for camp; it was a silent, diligent effort not to feel what we were both feeling. I drove her home when the day was done, and as I pulled up outside her house, she put her arms around me. We sat together for a long time, both crying… As a loving mother herself, she understood my loss. Ned was leaving home, not to return. What was I going to do with all the love I had for him? (p.167)

In this poem Connie Post talks about her son, Thomas, who was placed away from home at age six:

Writing You

I was writing you a letter
Today.

I neatly sealed the envelope
And slowly put a stamp on.

While writing the address,
I realized I couldn't remember
The zip code
Of where you now live.

I looked it up in the address book,
And all of the sudden,
Your name written in pencil
Took its place on that page,

And I just couldn't understand
Why my six year old boy,
Had a different address than mine.

Handsome buildings, attractive grounds, good programs, and caring staff who make their new clients welcome are all critical—without them the parents might not have agreed to have their son or daughter live with that agency. The usual long process of making the move was a lot of work. But when the high drama of the move is over and the parents go home, the heartbreak can be unexpectedly powerful.

Professionals serving these families need to be especially sensitive and supportive at this time. The literature on supports for people who've lost loved ones can provide useful suggestions for grieving parents whose child has recently been "placed." For families with a longer need, if the published material on the workings of grief is not enough to sustain and guide them, there are grief counselors who might be of great service.

References

Barron, J. and Barron, S. (2002) *There's a Boy in Here.* Arlington, TX: Future Horizons.

Christopher, B. and Christopher, W. (1989) *Mixed Blessings.* Nashville, TN: Abingdon Press.

Post, C. (1993) *Letting Go.* www.poetrypost.com

TWENTY-SIX

Toshiko Lyons

Life with Edmund began with the obstetrician's enthusiastic, "A prince has been born!" It was an April day 39 years ago in San Francisco, a city named after St. Francis of Assisi. I am devoted to the saint, and San Francisco was the birthplace of my husband. We were very grateful for our second picture-perfect baby. Edmund's brother Arthur, 18 months older, was happy to be with someone so soft who giggled at his touch.

Our peaceful life continued, with both children healthy and happy. I made sure that their check-ups were up to date, and they always received an "A+" from our pediatrician. We had a great time seeing the sights and visiting people all around the Bay area, and occasionally we'd take long vacations in the US or Mexico.

As the months went by, we noticed that Edmund was not developing the way his brother had. His reactions to the world and people around him were very different from his brother's. He preferred not to be kissed, hugged, or touched. He was happiest left alone. My husband Ed and I thought he was just independent.

Edmund was about two and a half when his father's job assignment took us to the Philippines, where our new life started with the excitement of the birth of our third child, our "little princess." Arthur was delighted with his new baby sister. Edmund showed some interest and seemed happy, but his real interest was intently focused on the movement of the wheels of his new toy Tonka school bus—if I let him, he'd continue moving those wheels all day.

We lived in one of five village compounds in the Makati area, a suburb of Manila. The village was made up of well-to-do Philippino families, foreign diplomats, businessmen, and US government employees like us. We had three domestic helpers and a gardener. Many American families lived in our village compound, so we never felt isolated. We mothers would often visit each other and our children would play together. Our days were centered around them, arranging lots of play-dates for our nursery-school children, and they could play at friend's homes or on playgrounds without always being attended by *ya-yas* (nannies).

There was a Montessori School in the next village compound, and we enrolled Edmund in their nursery program. About a week later, the teacher called asking us to have him examined by the ear, nose, and throat specialist. She gave us a referral to see the top specialist in Manila. She said Edmund was different from the other children that she'd been caring for over the years.

The specialist couldn't find anything physically wrong with Edmund, so the teacher recommended that he be examined by a psychiatrist. My husband and I thought she was asking a little much, but since her concern was so sincere, we decided to follow her advice.

Over the next several months Edmund went through test after test by several US military psychiatrists and Philippine physicians. Ed wanted him to be examined at a noted neuropsychiatric clinic in California. We took him there, but were disappointed that they didn't have answers either. However, one of the specialists who examined Edmund mentioned that he "could possibly be a borderline childhood schizophrenic." All this time I'd refused to believe there was anything seriously wrong with him; he was about three years old, his toilet training had been finished a year and a half earlier, and he was physically healthy. He could run and walk, and he loved to listen to the music of the great composers like Beethoven, Brahms, and Chopin, as well as Broadway musical songs.

The California specialist recommended a psychiatrist where we lived. He mentioned that she'd been a student of a "noted psychiatrist" in the States, and that she'd practiced in the US for many years. We had no knowledge of this "noted psychiatrist," but we followed the recommendation.

On our return to the Philippines, the staff and teachers of the Montessori School agreed to have Edmund only if someone he knew and trusted accompanied him each day. So I started to attend half-day classes with him. It went on like this for six months, and he was happy. But it was taking too much time away from Arthur and Kathy, my other children. They were in the good hands of loving Philippine helpers, but I wanted to have more time to spend with them, too. So we hired a young college graduate to accompany Edmund to the Montessori School each day. This worked well for everyone. She was a loving and compassionate person, and he liked her very much.

We started family therapy with the recommended psychiatrist. After several visits my husband felt that it was a waste of his time, so he stopped, but I continued seeing the psychiatrist along with Edmund. I was exasperated, wanting to get to the bottom of this. Ed and I had heated arguments on the matter of Edmund, but otherwise our life in the Philippines was happy and peaceful. We lived amid abundant natural beauty, and the people were good. We spent time in the mountains in the hot season, and our children were thriving. Arthur was attending International School. He enjoyed all outdoor sports—swimming, tennis, golf, etc. Kathy enjoyed her friends, from all parts of the world. Edmund overcome his fear of the water and learned to swim from a gentle pool attendant. He even enjoyed jumping off the high board, and he had an English Terrier that he loved to play with.

We believed that Edmund could overcome whatever the problem was. But as he grew older, we were gradually forced to recognize how deeply different his behavior was. The time came for us to return to the US, so we researched the best Special Education public school programs. One of these schools was in northern Virginia, where my husband's office was located, so we moved there.

It was sad to leave the Philippines. On the way back to the US, we stopped in Japan to visit my parents. Immediately Edmund got very excited when he saw his grandfather. They had an amazing connection, and it was a joy to watch. In the middle of the night he'd quietly get out of his own bed and go crawl in bed with his grandfather. He was then seven, and he'd never done anything like that before. He had always wanted to sleep alone. Another shocking part of this was the fact that my father had always been a very stern and strict person. Before this, I'd never seen a tender side in him.

As soon as we settled in Virginia, Edmund had to go through tests and medical observation in order to be placed in a school. I remember vividly when the devastating conclusion was reached in a psychiatrist's office:

"Autistic. Cause unknown!" These were words that resounded in my ears forever afterward. Edmund was then placed in the autistic children's class at a regular public elementary school.

Edmund and I met his teacher, a strong, tall woman with a New York accent. She greeted him by squatting down and saying, "Hello Edmund!" Then she said, "Come with me and meet your new friends. Mother, please stay outside the classroom. You can observe through the one-way glass on the door."

He cried and didn't want to let go of me, but the teacher somehow managed to take him into the classroom. (I still don't know how she did it without force.) This tall, powerful-looking woman turned out to be a caring and very gentle person. She would tell me about her students in such an affectionate and loving way. She would also explain typical autistic behaviors to me, and her presence became both comforting and helpful to me. I felt that I learned so much more from her than from any of the specialists we'd seen over the years.

This teacher, Mrs. Debbie Masnik, had a profound affect on Edmund. She helped him to make eye contact for the first time, and encouraged us to talk to him at his eye level. We were often invited to visit her and her husband at their home. Edmund enjoyed their company, and he especially enjoyed feeding their pets.

We moved a couple more times before moving to Japan. In Japan we discovered that the educational program was not what we'd been led to expect. The Special Education program of the Department of Defense School was not adequate for an autistic student. They struggled to understand his situation, but couldn't seem to figure it out or diagnose it. There was only one person, a speech therapist, who was able to communicate with both Edmund and us. We decided to seek help elsewhere. Years earlier we'd heard of the Musashino Higashi School in Tokyo, but we didn't consider it then because it was a Japanese school, and we thought the language barrier would be a problem. But at this point we were desperate. We went to meet Dr. Kitahara, the principal and founder, and we asked if we could put Edmund under her guidance. She was hesitant because of his age. He was 19 years old at the time. Dr. Kitahara's "Daily Life Therapy" is geared toward younger children; but she sympathized with us and made an exception, agreeing to accept him on a trial basis. At the same time, she made it very clear that she was not a miracle worker.

Miracle or not, two months later Edmund was performing the American National Anthem as the flag of the United States was raised in front of thousands of people in a huge auditorium. It was an amazing sight! We all cried and I noticed that everyone was crying with us.

Dr. Kitahara's "Daily Life Therapy," a highly structured program for children with autism, was profoundly helping Edmund! Its emphasis is on compassion, respect, and establishing trust between teachers and students. Dr. Kitahara and the entire staff were really working as one to accomplish what they did in a short time.

Edmund and I commuted to school by train and bus. It took two hours just to go one way, but the distance and the crowded train rides didn't matter. Eventually the Boston Higashi School in Massachusetts was opened (1987), and he joined an international group of students there. He stayed for a little over a year. Dr. Kitahara was training him to be a teacher's aide for the young children. Sadly, when he reached 22, he had to leave the school because they didn't have a program for autistic adults. Dr. Kitahara tried very hard to allow Edmund to remain there, but the state laws had to be followed.

Dr. Kitahara is no longer with us, but we still feel her spirit. Both the Tokyo and Boston Higashi Schools continue to grow stronger, and can't help but feel her presence. Even now I feel that her "Daily Life Therapy" was the best way to reach Edmund, and to bring out his potential and his joy in living.

As time passed we found ourselves facing another big challenge. My husband was recovering from two cancer operations, and since he had to retire, we moved back to Virginia, where Edmund tried some sheltered workshops. Many hard-working staff tried to help him, but he began to show his frustration, since the programs were not specifically designed for autistic adults (as they grow older, it gets increasingly difficult to find programs geared toward them). All too often adults with autism are medicated into submission, and warehoused. We did not want that for Edmund. We used every means of networking, and with the help of Dr. Rimland we were very fortunate to find Bittersweet Farms in Whitehouse, Ohio. It is one of the few facilities in the United States that offers programs specifically geared for autistic adults.

Dr. Rimland knew the founder of the community and arranged for us to meet with her, Mrs. Betty Ruth Kay. We were very happy to find a place where Edmund would be cared for by an extremely well-meaning staff. It was becoming more difficult for me to care for both Edmund and my husband, who was fighting both lung and brain cancer.

Edmund spent 16 years at the community, actively involved with the programs they offered. But as time went on, he began to show frustration, sometimes violently. He was given medication, which didn't help his behavior. His weight increased because of the medication. I began to be concerned about both his behavior and his physical condition.

When I realized the seriousness of Edmund's diagnosis 34 years ago, I was bombarded with feelings of anger, helplessness, and grief, but I no longer felt that way when I decided to bring Edmund home after my husband died. I felt like a beginner in a motherhood class. I continued to seek advice from Dr. Rimland. Edmund has been living with me for a year and a half now, without medication, and he is back to his normal weight. He's been on the vitamin B6 therapy that was recommended by Dr. Rimland. We spend almost every day at a nearby YMCA; Edmund was chosen as member of the month last summer. He continues to enjoy participating in the Special Olympics.

Edmund is a very gentle, fragile individual. Because of his nature, he's easily hurt. Although he's considered high-functioning, he has a lot of difficulty in many areas. It may seem that he understands situations or what is said, but this is often not the case. To help him adjust smoothly to any changes, the changes need to be clearly and explicitly explained ahead of time. Both verbal and written explanations help. He feels hurt when he's corrected, criticized, or repeatedly prompted. Sometimes it doesn't even matter whether the tone of voice is soft or loud. He gets embarrassed easily, and that upsets him very much.

Another key in helping Edmund is the importance of praising him and reinforcing what he does right. No matter how small either his action or the reinforcement is, it's still a step in helping him to adjust smoothly.

Edmund is constantly seeking companionship with kind people. The best example of this would be Mother Theresa. Her life and her being were wonderful examples of the firm compassion and self-discipline that underprivileged or disabled people need. Establishing trust with people around him is extremely important to Edmund. It helps him to remove the armor that he has built.

I am grateful for the opportunity and experience that I'm receiving in this lifetime. I've just begun to understand the true meaning of love. Unconditional love from Edmund, the people around him, and from families and friends, as well as the wonderful love and support of my late husband Ed.

Life is truly a series of lessons, and Edmund has taught me and continues to teach me so much. Caring for him has opened doors for me to meet so many wonderful people. I now accept the words Mother Theresa told me in Japan. Holding my hands firmly she said, "You have a treasure in your family. Take care of it!"

TWENTY-SEVEN

Sally Graham

My son Edward was diagnosed autistic at age three. The following year we met the Rimlands and became involved with a newly formed organization, the National Society for Autistic Children. Although he had delayed speech and still has difficulty with social skills, Ed is very high functioning, thanks to many dedicated and caring teachers and therapists, as well as a family which supports and cares for him.

Ed got his first bicycle when he was about seven. He's owned and ridden a bike ever since, to work and to the store, and to places he just likes to visit.

When he was in his teens he started biking to places in the local Thomas Map Guide. For several years he visited sites that were listed alphabetically, week by week. Later on, he enjoyed going back to his old schools and to houses where he'd lived, visiting one or more on Saturdays, some of them fifteen to twenty miles away. He still enjoys doing this, although it's more of an effort these days since he's physically not in as good shape as he used to be. He's a very careful cyclist; he always wears a helmet and follows the rules of the toad. When a car cuts him off, or in his estimation is reckless, it makes him very upset.

One day when he was 16, Ed announced at dinner that he'd need 40 dollars in the morning. When we asked why, he told us that he was going to take driving lessons. He'd been taking Driver's Education at his high school and realized that in order to get his license, he'd need behind-the-wheel experience, so he took it upon himself to check the Yellow Pages and make the arrangements. He passed the test and got his license!

He's had his own car—his most prized possession—for quite a few years now. Most of his trips are less than twenty miles, but he did make the journey from San Diego to Santa Barbara by himself once. (That took years off my life!) As with his bicycle riding, he's extremely cautious, and is careful to drive defensively. When he parks, he always gets out and checks that he's the correct distance from the curb before locking the car, and of course, he's particular about oil changes, and service when necessary.

I must admit that I worry, as all mothers do when their children drive, but at the same time I'm glad that Ed has reached this level of independence. He will always need some guidance and help at times, and this is a source of frustration to him. The more he accomplishes on his own, the less he wants to be monitored, maybe because he is now a man in his forties. It's so important to him that he manages on his own, and he's shown us that he's very capable in many ways.

TWENTY-EIGHT

Lawrence Stream

Lawrence Wyatt was born September 21, 1957. We were subjected to that same defamatory Bettelheim bilge about the "Refrigerator Mother" cause of autism as everyone else who had autistic kids born back then.

We call him Larry Wyatt or LW. In very early photos he appears happy and perfectly normal, but his delayed speech alerted us to some major disability. He did manage to communicate though, even in his speechless state. Once, when he became very angry with his mother, he led her to the garbage can and indicated that she should deposit herself there!

He became a skilled twirler of everything from bottle caps to garbage can lids. He liked steps, so I built a stile for him, suitable for going over a low imaginary fence. He was intrigued with octagonal shapes, and stop signs were one of the first things he drew. He had a very limited diet: milk, Belgian waffles, Captain Crunch cereal, and Bugles, the snack food. I don't recall any problems in toilet training, but his diet was such that an enema became part of the daily routine. Is megacolon somehow associated with autism?

LW was seen at the Child Study Center of the University of Oklahoma Medical School. After three years of studying him they decided that LW was a very interesting enigma, and he was placed on Mellaril, an anti-psychotic. He then spent a year at the disability school of the Oklahoma

City (OKC) system. The headmaster of Casady, the city's most prestigious private school, had a Down's syndrome son, and he was given a study grant to determine whether teachers who were not specifically trained to teach the disabled could function in that capacity. LW was selected as a student in this study group, a very lucky turn of events. The teachers were dedicated, and LW became their prize student. Somewhere along the way, he got off the Mellaril and onto a mega-multi-vitamin regimen.

One story about him at that time concerns a local amusement park called Wedgewood. They had a theme song that was played frequently on radio and TV, and LW would hum the tune whenever he wanted to go there, but one day it didn't produce the result he wanted, and LW then uttered his first complete sentence, "I want to go to Wedgewood, and I want to go now." My startled wife Milly immediately obliged.

Speaking still seems to be a major chore to LW. In answer to a simple question, he must first clear his throat and get some sort of mental mechanism in gear even to say, "Yes" or, "No." In response to a verbal command or request, he must first repeat the order, to get the mechanism started. In stressful situations the mechanism may break down, he might not understand what's said to him, and he might have increased difficulty in speaking. It's unfortunate that many people, even professionals who deal with autism, base their impressions of people solely on conversational skills.

The second story involves Milly, who had a particularly heavy schedule on September 21 in 1965 or 1966, when LW was turning eight or nine. She'd decided that she didn't have time to arrange a birthday party at school for him. She rationalized that he probably didn't even know it was his birthday. But as she went by his room early that morning, she heard a small voice singing, "Happy birthday to me…"—she immediately put the arrangement of a party at the top of her list of things to do that morning.

For a time LW attended Casady in the mornings and Timberridge in the afternoon. Later he attended Timberridge all day. It was a school started by psychologists for youngsters with emotional disturbances. Students who successfully did their school work and had no emotional outbursts were given special privileges: a camping trip to Arkansas, a trip to Six Flags amusement park in Dallas or Silver Dollar City in Branson, Missouri. LW always qualified. He was a model student, cooperative in whatever therapeutic regime was introduced, and in every institution there would be one or two teachers who became his champion and long-standing friend.

Timberridge was designed to accommodate students for a year or two until they "got their heads on straight." LW was the only one in his group to finish the schooling they offered, and there was a graduation of sorts. Timberridge provided LW with driver's education, and he passed his driving test on his first try.

From this point on we had no clear educational goals in mind, and our guidance tended to wander aimlessly. LW attended four institutions, passed a smattering of different courses, and had private tutoring in math and English. We decided that getting his GED might be in order, and he took a course with this goal in mind. He did well, but it was suggested he might consider additional tutoring in reading to make certain he passed on his initial test.

LW reads extensively about things that interest him. He writes letters that aren't literary masterpieces, but are grammatically correct, with no spelling errors. (A trip, no matter how short, is his opportunity to fire off a bunch of postcards.) LW does well with facts, but not concepts. He knows the order of the planets and their distance from the sun, but he doesn't know why it might be harder to breathe in Leadville than Louisville. He came up with the thought that if you're standing on the North Pole, all directions are South. In the best autistic savant tradition, he knows the birth and death dates of the entire family—grandparents, uncles, aunts, cousins—and he knows the years we took specific trips.

In 1976 a letter from the Autism Research Institute (ARI) informed us that Dr. William Philpott had opened a psychiatric practice in OKC, and that he had an unusual approach to the treatment of autism, in case we were interested. We were. In short order LW underwent a four-day fast, followed by a four-day rotation diet intended to calm food allergies. He improved immediately.

He couldn't stay on his diet on trips, and after about ten days off it he would become increasingly lethargic, fearful, and negative. In one sense, this diet was a curse as well as a blessing, because he became home-kitchen bound. For instance, he couldn't attend Ozark College in Clarksville, Arkansas, where they had a special program for the educationally challenged, because of dietary considerations.

It's interesting that Dr. Philpott thought the rotation diet should be used in rehabilitation of prisoners, just as, for other reasons, Dreyfus thought Dilantin should be given a trial in the prison population. Dr. Philpott was so pleased with LW's progress that he had Milly and LW appeared with him later that year when he lectured in Houston. We later went to St. Petersburg, Florida, where Dr. Philpott relocated, for further testing in 1983 and 1987.

In 1992 we went to Texas for auditory training that was definitely beneficial. LW said the "scratchy background noise" disappeared. Milly said the lines on his face lessened, he appeared more relaxed, and he had a sudden resumption of his artistic activity. He completed two pictures on the spot, one of which he sold, and he gave the other to people at the training center.

We were also referred to an optometrist who was interested in the distortion of visual input in people with autism. He said that LW's diplopia hadn't been corrected, that his brain refused to be confused by the input of his second eye and simply turned it off. Since then he's been fitted with prism glasses.

In 1991 LW began seeing Dr. Diane Mobley, a nearby autism expert, and continued every second week for about two years. Since 1993 he's been working with a speech therapist on a weekly basis. In 1995 he began seeing Dr. Fred Weber, a psychiatrist, who put him on Luvox after I saw an article suggesting it might be helpful in treating perseveration. After several years it was discontinued because of weight gain. Over the years he's had successful psychotherapy dealing with his fears of elevators and of air flights.

LW had no formal art training until 1975, but he was already producing colored pencil drawings of mountain scenery. We'd been taking Colorado vacations with him since he was about eight, but our first trip to the Alps, the subject of most of his paintings, wasn't until he was 18. His paintings have been displayed at our church, two hospitals, at art shows in OKC, Norman, and Edmond (two nearby cities), at two local colleges, Casady School book fair, OKC art museums, Greens Country Club, and at a local art gallery. He was also Artist of the Month three times at a local cafeteria chain.

He usually rises around 10:00 a.m. and fixes Rice Krispies or waffles for his breakfast. Some days he goes to the YMCA for workouts. For lunch he goes to one of four Mexican restaurants in turn. Tuesday night he bowls and has some nachos at the bowling alley. Two Friday nights a month I play bridge at a country club, and he usually has dinner with me at the club. On other nights we eat at home, and he usually requests fish sticks. Tuesday mornings he has an art class with a neighborhood teacher. Every other Tuesday afternoon he has a 30-minute session with a psychiatrist. On

Wednesday afternoon LW spends an hour with the speech therapist. One Friday night a month he goes to a local astronomy club meeting. He attends church faithfully, and he's developed friendships with a few people who have been able to establish rapport with him. Sunday afternoons he goes to a city park for a nature walk, or other programs with a naturalist. Here again, he's developed close friendships with the staff. For several years, he attended weekly sessions at a therapeutic horseback-riding center. This was designed for children, but LW continued it until his increasing weight proved more than an average horse could bear.

In the afternoons and evenings, when not otherwise occupied, LW withdraws to his room. He emerges to take a bath every night, and after I retire he takes over the living room to watch the Leno show on TV and one or more of his extensive collection of videotapes.

One autistic trait that LW does *not* exhibit is an obsession with orderliness; he's like a teenager, and his room looks like a disaster area. My next goal is to get him more involved in housekeeping: operating a clothes washer and dryer, the dishwasher, and rearranging the household clutter.

Over 25 years ago I realized that my son's long-term care might be a problem, so I bought mutual funds under the Gifts to Minors Act. These grew enough that he wasn't eligible for disability aid, but he did qualify as my social security dependent when I retired. I opened a checking account for him, and obtained Visa and gasoline credit cards in his name so he could establish a credit history of his own. I usually give him $20 each day before he goes out to eat, and then he does some personal shopping. If he doesn't have enough cash he uses his Visa. One time he bought a TV set for Milly's birthday all on his own, and arranged to have it delivered. Usually he writes a check to his art teacher and his speech therapist, and for his credit card charges.

Many years ago, we did some estate planning to maximize the amount that could be placed in a trust for LW's future care, and to minimize inheritance taxes. We've managed our finances with care, and there should be more than adequate funds for his future needs.

Our nearest relatives are two nieces, Barbara and Bonnie. They live about 75 miles from OKC. Barbara and her attorney husband and our local attorney are all involved as trustees. I suppose it would be best if LW ends up in an assisted living facility with optional dining arrangements. The only thing I wish to avoid is some sort of institution. This would be the end of the freedom his car driving provides, and it would crush him emotionally. There would be advantages if he were in a smaller community and closer to his cousins, but this would mean severing the social ties he's established in OKC. I think he could manage by himself here with a little help—renewing his driver's license, paying insurance, getting new car tags, having the oil changed, filing income tax returns, etc. He's a member of AAA, but getting someone to understand what he's saying might be a problem if he needed roadside assistance.

LW loves to travel. We've been to Switzerland five times, the Canadian Rockies three times, the inside passage to Alaska twice, Hawaii, the South Island of New Zealand, the Panama Canal, and every state in the western US. (It makes it a bit difficult to arrange a brand new itinerary.) He still talks about going back to school, but I suspect what he really has in mind is meeting some blonde coed who wants to marry him.

Milly had major problems with her memory for almost four years before she died. LW would say, "It's no fun having a mixed-up mother." This was an expression of the anguish he felt about losing an integral part of his very best friend. Milly, bless her memory, never took exception to his seemingly thoughtless remark, as if she knew what he was really trying to say. The last year she was more desperately ill, and I did what I could to prepare him for the inevitable. LW visited her faithfully during the times she was in the hospital or in a nursing home; he often went alone to see her when he went for lunch, and also later in the day with me. She was at the funeral home several days between her death and interment, and whenever I went there to attend to details, he'd go with me and spend the whole time in the viewing room with Milly. When they asked about a photograph for the newspaper obituary, LW immediately spoke up that he had one, and produced it, and a very appropriate choice it was. Since her death, several times he's said, "I sure miss Mother." I believe he carries that photo with him, and a laminated copy of the obituary. I don't believe either of us will completely recover from her loss.

TWENTY-NINE

Maxine Richards

When Randy was diagnosed as autistic at about age three, I did what most parents do; I set about learning everything I could to help him. I'd like to tell what experiences were most helpful to both of us.

What helped me get on the right track from the very beginning was the doctor who diagnosed Randy. When I asked him, "What's autism?" he said, "We don't really know, but it's nothing you've done." I thought it was a strange thing to say at the time, but it was a great confidence builder when we later faced some of the "treatments" for autism. My knowledge expanded as I read Dr. Rimland's *Infantile Autism*.

I'll always be thankful for my parents and their wonderful wisdom and common sense. They were a great support whenever my confidence faltered, like when a mental health professional told me, "You're using black magic on Randy," because I didn't stick to the psychiatric model of autism. (With the vitamin regimen, his perpetual runny nose was cured; I don't think biomedicine is exactly "black magic.")

Parents have been conditioned to think professionals know best, and we tend to give them authority over our autistic children. I believe that parents know their own children better than anyone else. After all, we live with them fulltime in their real context, and have observed them far more deeply than the professionals. We need to be more confident in this knowledge—it certainly has been hard-earned!

A group of parents can do wonders armed with this confidence. For example, it was a group of parents from Morgan Center that visited their local state Representative; they requested, and were granted, legislation that funded summer school for special education students. It can also be as simple as the parent I saw who had the courage born of this confidence to wear a T-shirt that said "Respite Care Prevents Institutionalization" at a Sacramento hearing.

One of the first tools to help me get Randy on a learning track was structure, without which it was very difficult to keep him focused on a task. I learned the value not only of structure, but also how to be consistent with it and then to introduce reasonable changes.

Playing to Randy's handicap of wanting things smooth, in order, or lined up, he was given Montessori toys like the broad stair and the tower. Then jigsaw puzzles with individual pieces, i.e. tree, ball, shapes, etc. Verbal prompts were given with each piece. We used conditioning (quick reward) for putting the piece in the right place and for repeating the word. Next were picture books with pictures of objects on each page with the matching written word. Colored papers were matched with verbal prompts. Good structure, good lesson plans, and lots of hard work. It was so great to see Randy "get it" and become more able to make some sense out of his world.

As changes were made in structured lessons, there were carry-over-in-action events such as matching words with what was happening, e.g. "Up—up the stairs." The reward system in conditioning is important. Randy responded only to material rewards (food) at first. Later, social rewards like praise and smiles were meaningful to him. In my opinion, some behaviorists can be too rigid in their practice of rewards or punishment. "All behavior is learned," they say, but that doesn't mean the parents have taught the bizarre behavior! Holding to too-strict conditioning methods may close other avenues of help. For example, one day Randy was upset and was displaying his temper. My good friend, Linda Urquart, said to him, "Randy, do you feel bad? Do you need a hug?" Then she gave him a hug. And it worked! He calmed down because his feelings had been validated.

Parents of autistic kids have a wealth of common sense. Having a support system of other parents is priceless.

For parents of school-age children, the most valuable tool is knowing your child's rights under the law (in California, PL-142) and how to use them. The value of getting a well-written Individual Educational Program was the key to getting Randy on the right track for progress toward his potential. This was not an easy thing to do, but perseverance paid off. I must give credit to BACH (Bay Area Coalition for the Handicapped), a parent organization that gave workshops on IEPs (Individualized Education Programs).

There are two legal steps I took that I feel confident will protect my son in the future. One was becoming his payee: an easy process through Social Security. The other was getting conservatorship of him, which I believe gives me more authority because my consent is often required regarding his life activities.

Above all, I believe that being able to have a sense of humor with Randy has enhanced our relationship. For example, when we went shopping during the time when he was obsessed with hammers, when he took one off display and hooked it on his belt we'd say, "You can't do that," or, "It costs too much money." Months later, when he patted a female staff member's behind and she said, "Randy, you can't do that," he of course echoed, "It costs too much money!"

Randy is now 45 years old and living in a PACE (Pacific Autism Center for Education) group home with five other guys. His day program is the Morgan Center for Autism Spectrum Disorders adult program. Both facilities have high standards of service to autistic people. Randy is fairly well adjusted, and seems happy in both places.

THIRTY

Arlene J. Paster

We started our first parent group in 1957 because we wanted accurate scientific diagnoses and also public education for our children. Our children were adults before we and the other parents who'd joined us were successful in this. Known as Jay Nolan Community Services, we first merged with parent groups in the East who later merged with the Mental Health Association. That didn't work well, and so we happily merged with the Autism Society of America once we learned of its existence.

I think that the needs of the children with autism who are growing up now are different from the needs of our generation of kids when they were young. Today's early diagnosis, early childhood education, speech, occupational therapy, and other interventional therapies make a great difference in functional abilities.

Our son David spent many years in California State Hospitals (he was at Camarillo for 21 years), then we bought a small townhouse for him shortly after the earthquake ten years ago. He has 24-hour caretakers. Two men share caretaking duties five days a week and, a third man shares the weekends. David is non-verbal, and indicates any unhappiness with miserably inappropriate behaviors. Nobody he doesn't like stays with him long. We are really fortunate that the two main caretakers have been with him for all ten years, and one was with him at the group home where he lived before. They're wonderful, and David loves them. He never smiled in all the years he was at Camarillo, but he smiles a lot now.

I think our low-functioning adults could use some daily activities suited to their abilities and needs, but they're not welcome at community gym programs. My son didn't know how to climb stairs when he moved into his home. He could have used a good adaptive Physical Education program. I paid for a music therapist at Northridge University for a while, and he loved her program, but she soon switched to working with young children, and there was no one to take her place. The state Regional Center isn't too happy if our kids just visit parks and shopping malls or stay at home, but then they don't support employment programs, whereas most Jay Nolan clients are employed in some way. (Most are a little younger than David, and have some education.) Most of the parents of our clients say, "Thank God for Jay Nolan Center!" Our greatest concern is keeping our program adequately funded.

As a special education teacher in our valley (Los Angeles Unified School District) I saw what a great difference early education made for our children and others with developmental disabilities. Yes, there were autistic children in some of our schools, though we were told not to call them that, when they still weren't legally there. Since the time that David was very young, the children in his age group have had many labels—atypical, schizophrenic, mentally ill, neurologically handicapped, multiply handicapped, ADD, ADHD, "crazy," EMR (educable mentally retarded), TMR (trainable mentally retarded), emotionally disturbed, severely emotionally disturbed, etc. Now they're all part of the Autism Spectrum. (Sounds good to me.)

I'm concerned that parents of children who are scattered to many schools and all sorts of classes aren't getting it together to plan for their child's future life. All parents hope that by some miracle, or by ensuring as many enrichment programs as they can, their child will grow up no longer autistic. Future plans take years to formulate and realize, and like us, all parents get older. I'm afraid that for these younger families, there will be nothing available when they need it. I always remember what Ann Wendt, former Director of United Cerebral Palsy, told me years ago, "Every child should have the right to grow up and move away from home."

I must add here that my grandson has a diagnosis of PDD-NOS. He's doing fairly well in a regular first-grade class with lots of help. Before first grade, he was in speech and language classes. Given David's lack of any speech, it's a surprise that my grandson tests highest in expressive language.

One more thing I'd like to comment on: when David was at Camarillo and Reagan was governor of California, our children were fed huge amounts of unnecessary drugs. We parents weren't allowed the right to "just say no," a special irony. Some died. David got *grand mal* seizures that nobody in the hospitals could control. They had to call in outside experts. Today my son and others are still suffering the side effects of all those drugs. Last year I had to fight Denti-Cal, the California state dental program, to get David a permanent bridge. He has gum and bone damage that made him lose his front teeth. I won on an appeal after writing to every local politician. Some of our other Camarillo graduates are having the same problems and losing their teeth, according to those parents I'm still in touch with, but I bet there are more.

THIRTY-ONE

Mary Laird Flanagan

Chris was a most beautiful baby, born when I was 23 and knew nothing about babies. But by his first birthday we knew something was terribly wrong. When he was 18 months old, I diagnosed him myself from a description in a psychology book from the public library.

Now he's 49, low-functioning, nonverbal, and non-aggressive, but he's a behavioral problem because he's addicted to eating cigarette butts, and will act dangerously to try to get them.

His teeth and gums are his biggest physical problem because he can't tell people if they're hurting. Years ago a tooth abscess caused him to break out behaviorally, losing all the progress he'd made.

Of course I was told I'd *made* Chris autistic—another cold, rejecting, "Refrigerator Mother" of that era, so my first daughter was a lifesaver for me—a total cuddler and communicator. She was born 17 months after him, and I never worried for a moment that she could be autistic too.

When I became pregnant for the fourth time and there was no help for Chris or me or the rest of the family, we put him into a residential placement that looked promising. He seemed happy there, but he made no significant improvement and was asked to leave. Four other placements followed, some good, some not.

Chris started taking Zyprexa five years ago, and for the first time in his life, he isn't tormented by crippling anxiety. I can finally say he is happy.

The staff where he now lives enjoy him—he teases like a naughty two-year-old.

Do I think his life has been worthwhile to him? No. He's suffered too much, and he is so dependent on the quality of the people working with him that I'll always fear for his well-being.

For the last ten years he's been in a residence at the Developmental Disabilities Institute in Suffolk County, New York, and also in its day program. He's been blessed in the quality of the residential staff, but the day program is a problem because the pay is inadequate, and so are most of the staff.

What have I learned? For parents who want to find out what's best for their children and how to access it, get involved. Join the ASA (Autism Society of America) and other organizations. Learn the disability laws, and the names of all the people in your area who administer them. I joined and then became president of the Long Island ASA chapter, and started a small service organization with them. Everyone in the local office of the state Office of Mental Retardation and Developmental Disabilities knew who I was, which groups I was connected with, and eventually, what my needs were for Chris. Get to know all of your local politicians. If you're lucky, as I was, you'll find a smart, kind, and well-connected representative or senator who can help get things done for your child, and everyone else's as well.

Visit all programs, talk to all the parents you can, read the books and journals. Avoid the weird promises of miracle changes. Be rich, or work for a large business in your area. Or connect with someone who is, because government and private agencies respond to money and power. For a while, my husband had a job that made a lot of money. We bought and renovated Chris's group home ourselves. We helped the start-up organization. Things are different now, but we still make a point of giving a noticeable sum to the organization that cares for him.

We have a trust fund for him that his sisters will administer when we're gone. It conforms to the current New York State law, so the money will not create a problem for his SSI funding.

A warning: one of my worst mistakes was to trust some other disability organizations and people, assuming they were honest with me. Funding grants are scarce and money even scarcer, so people will cheat you without apparent compunction. Working in the disability field does not make someone a good or honest person.

Best decision we made: joining the ASA. From other hard-working parents, I learned what I needed to do. And I met wonderful friends-for-life, other parents of autistic children. Our sons are all grown now and all very different, but that doesn't matter in our friendship for each other. Volunteering for ASA Information and Referral for ten years was also good. Helping younger parents who'd just discovered that their child was autistic made me feel useful. I didn't want their children to be lost into autism as mine was. I felt I made a difference. Those parents in turn helped me; the final New York State permission to open Chris's group home is something I owe to two mothers of little ones that I'd advised, who rolled up their sleeves for me in return.

I couldn't have done what I have without my steadfast and hard-working husband. We've been married for 50 years. Our three daughters have delighted and consoled us. Both our granddaughter and our grandson are wonderful, and not autistic.

Autism is a terrible, destructive blight, and there were times when I didn't think I'd survive. But in many ways we've been lucky, and much good has come our way.

THIRTY-TWO

Dr. and Mrs. William K. Henry

Before secretin

As our son Andrew grew to over six feet tall, at times he was too aggressive for my five-foot, three-inch wife to handle. We had to resort to medications to calm him down. I hate the very description of these drugs: sedatives and anti-psychotics, but it was all we had. The side effects were bad, but it was better than nothing. The bottom line was that he was not improving much on them, even with all the vitamin and herb therapies we were giving him.

Medications just were not the answer for us. These days stretched into months and years—the most grim and grievous times imaginable!

Enter secretin

About ten years ago I was in an herbal medical store exchanging some tablets that we were giving Andrew. The bonding agent on the lot was bad, and I was helping the owner take the tablets off his shelf with that specific lot number. As we busied ourselves we talked, and he mentioned that there would be a presentation on a breakthrough on autism on one of the early-morning news programs soon. I went home without much hope;

we'd been down this road a few times, following up on "breakthroughs," with little to show for it.

I worked late that night, into the early hours of the morning. As I was taking a break at about 3:00 a.m., an advertisement came on the TV about that very news show, mentioning that it would be on at 7:00 a.m. It was all about Parker Beck. I would have missed this had not, I believe, the Lord Jesus Christ energized me about the project at hand, so that I would stay up. I taped the show that morning, in awe of what was happening on the screen before my eyes. I showed the tape to my wife and we watched another news program presentation the next day, interviewing Victoria Beck, Parker's mother.

We showed the tape to our doctor and got the research and the testimony for him from the Autism Research Institute, and he agreed to administer the secretin since there were no known side effects. The results were astounding. Andrew has been off of the really heavy medications ever since. We've been the pioneers, so to speak, with a son as old as Andrew (he was born in 1976), and to us secretin is like a miracle! How great a miracle you ask? After the wonderful effects of the first infusion were beginning to ebb at the end of the second week, Andrew came to us and said, "Doctor! Shot!" He knew, he knew, he knew!!! It's similar to insulin for a diabetic—it's living! Because of secretin our world has become tolerable over the years, even joyful, including the marriage of our youngest son to our sweet daughter-in-law, along with the birth of our wonderful little grandson. Our youngest son has suffered much over the years along with Andrew, helping both us and his brother greatly, and loving him unconditionally.

So what have the changes been since starting secretin? His eye contact has improved dramatically. His affection level has gone up tremendously, from rejecting hugs to seeking them. His expressive vocabulary has increased. His desire to be among people is way up. All the things associated with the antisocial challenges of autism are slowly melting away. He seems so capable of many things; he seems so smart, but like a marvelous car stuck in neutral. He wants to be in our world now!

Why has the change taken place slowly? We're not sure. We operate with Andrew on the theory that autism is a person's response mechanism to the inability of the brain to process data about social relationships. We believe this causes fear, and that repetition is simply a way of coping with fear. Once he does something that helps him in a time of fear or uncertainty about social relations, he feels compelled to repeat it. This is slowly going away. We believe it's going slowly because he developed powerful emotional coping habits over all those years and, as we all know, habits are hard to break. This is why we believe that the earlier the intervention, the better. To that end, we also employed behavioral programs, allergy clinics, plus auditory training and years of speech therapy, all of which have proven helpful.

We've been confronted by several challenges with the use of secretin. First, there are two methods to give secretin: either IV infusion or transdermal; we've used both. Sometimes it appeared that infusions were less effective toward the end of the infusion period. That's when we began to supplement with the transdermal. We've monitored and increased his dosage as it has seemed needful; and we now are only using transdermal, which is much more effective, as the amount administered daily is constant, which keeps him "even."

Second, in most cases all types of secretin must be kept frozen until used. I've had to chase down a UPS truck because I knew the dry ice in the packaging was beginning to thaw. A small mistake in delivery or handling could have cost us over $250 at the time, much less the problem that we would be out of the secretin right at the next infusion date. Moreover, it's critical to use thawed secretin within 30 minutes. (We are told it is virtually worthless after that time.)

A third challenge has been finances. Secretin is supported by some insurance companies and not by others. We've known them to cover the administration of secretin, but not the purchase of the medication itself. The cost has been as high as $600 per month, plus doctor's fees for the infusion process alone. The Japanese source was the cheapest we found, at about $40 per month. Germany is also a source, but their price the last time we checked ran up to $1800 per month. Our current source, now in the States, charges us $3125.00 per month for nine vials of Secreflo®. Andrew's dosage requirements have increased over the years from four vials per month to nine. In addition, our cost for the compounding procedure is $500 per month.

Lastly, an infusion is much like an IV. A needle called a "butterfly" infusion must be placed in the vein. If possible, alternate infusion sites need to be used to keep scarring at a minimum. The least painful site is the crook of the elbow. Because of a potentially lethal staphylococcus infection two years ago, we've switched to the transdermal method, which has been life-changing and more than satisfactory medically.

There are several types of secretin available. We've found the most effective for our son is porcine secretin. It's had the most remarkable results for Andrew by far.

We receive the secretin in the nine vials, then a compounding pharmacist converts the medication to an ointment that is placed in an applicator and kept frozen until just minutes before use. We warm it to room temperature and, using a latex examination glove, we apply the ointment to a soft-tissue area where clothing will not rub it away. We're told that it must stay on the skin for at least 20 minutes to get maximum absorption. We're also told that where the blood vessels are closest to the skin are the optimum locations to apply the ointment. However, we have found that application to the neck has worked well.

Dosing was at first guesswork, and then from there we simply observed Andrew's behavior in order to adjust the dosage. We've had to adjust the regular dosage some six times over the ten years we have used secretin. It appears that the law of diminishing returns may be at work, because Andrew's size and weight have remained pretty much stable.

There've been times when Andrew was very irritable, either from lack of sleep, or he was sick, or was stung by a bee, etc. At those times, we've provided a small additional dose (about 10 percent of a regular syringe). Our observation is that this allows him to handle irritability without becoming overtly angry.

With secretin

We believe that secretin is Andrew's gateway to healing. Now, using behavioral modification, we're working to build his understanding of our consistent behavior and facial expressions. He's learning to imitate a smile, and to feel what we feel. It's become wonderful to him, so that now he's initiating smiling in order to get us to smile back, a major emotional milestone. Because of his age (now 31), we felt this was the important first step. In other words, we're trying to take the fear out of social relationships; his lack of ability to understand or predict was causing him a great deal of insecurity, and we hope that his increased understanding can help end repetitive coping behaviors, and that he might begin more complex forms of learning.

We owe much to Bernie Rimland for connecting us with the right people and encouraging us all along the way. Andrew began taking Super-Nu-Thera at the age of four, and still does. We also are very grateful to Steve Edelson for his compassion for Andrew since 1991.

Andrew has made great strides, and he has very far to go. We take it all one day at a time, just as God has told us to do. We now smile again and look to a bright future with our precious son whom we are honored to love and care for…we trust that, as Corrie ten Boom said, "The best is yet to come."

THIRTY-THREE

Francine M. Bernstein

Bradley left home at six years old, when a treatment center in Florida accepted him. (The promised cure was contingent on his being out of his home environment; the cold insinuation of this had by then become sadly familiar, but no less hurtful.) He returned to our home outside Chicago in 1969, when he was 11, and his repetitive gestures, lack of communication, and self-injurious behavior (SIB) persisted. With his growth and increased strength came the awful threat of serious injury to himself.

Our tax money still did not provide a public school classroom for our child. At that time the severely autistic were warehoused in the back wards of mental hospitals, so we felt fortunate to find a small private school that took a special interest in children like him. But when we dropped in to observe one day, we were appalled to find our Bradley tied to a chair in front of the class, his obvious incontinence adding insult to injury. My son had never wet himself before.

I became hysterical. The staff had not thought to give this child of mine the courtesy of a toilet break. To our dismay, this became a "Catch 22" that Brad would experience many times: "time out" in restraints did prevent head banging, but it also prevented learning. Unrestrained time-outs in confinement risked black eyes or a broken nose, from his head banging.

I desperately wanted a program for Bradley. Roz Oppenheim, whom I'd met in 1963 at an NSAC (National Society for Autistic Children) meeting, agreed to work on Brad's language deficiencies (Roz had meanwhile earned her MA in Special Education). We'd become friends through the years because of our sons' similar struggles—she also was the mother of an autistic son who was self-injurious. Public Law 94-142 had just been passed, so I suggested that Roz and I start a school of our own. We approached our respective school districts and the Illinois Department of Mental Health (IDMH) for funding. We wanted to create a more meaningful day program for the severely autistic.

We found a synagogue willing to rent its upper-floor classrooms. We set up a not-for-profit corporation that we named the "Rimland School for Autistic Children," after Bernard Rimland, the well-known authority on autism and the father of an affected teenage boy. We incorporated in September 1971, beginning with five clients, including Roz's son, Ethan, and my son, Bradley. Roz became the salaried teacher/director, and I was the pro bono bookkeeper. We were lucky to have Carol Ann Auclair, a classmate of Roz's who was a former nun and a certified high school teacher, volunteer to help Roz in the classroom.

Within a few short years my son became uncontrollable once more. His self-destructive head banging could impair his eyesight, but each effort to stop it failed, and Brad's self-injury escalated. In desperation, I tried a shocker. (Brad had shared a house with a person who injured himself. They used the shocker to deter it, which made learning new behaviors with positive rewards possible, so I knew it could have a positive effect.) By then Brad's father and I felt we'd exhausted all the possible so-called positive methods.

From its consistent application following head banging, Brad was programmed to stop and take a pause when he saw the shocker. It could only be applied on the buttocks, legs, or arms. The shocker couldn't make him *do* a task. It made him *available* to be put through a task. Then we could reward him with positive reinforcement. Over time, Brad could do multiple steps without a reward for each step. We could see that the goal of independence could be attained.

We requested that IDMH/DD (Illinois Dept. of Mental Health and Developmental Disabilities) representatives meet with our SIB consultant, Dr. Nate Azrin. Together, we designed a program of positive reinforcement that ultimately extinguished Bradley's self-injurious behavior. Dr. Azrin and the IDMH/DD policymakers agreed on a behavioral modification program with the use of the shocker, with the application restricted to task-avoidance head banging. The school staff had to document its use. Observation and periodic review were required. Finally, Bradley had some consistency.

Meanwhile, Rimland School enjoyed continued success with the development of life skills and limited academics for the severely autistic. Enrollment grew. Classrooms were added. Fundraising improved. Soon classes needed to be replaced with vocational programs. Our son and his older classmates were well into their teens; as young men and women, they needed to experience living outside their parents' homes. We thought about what arrangements Bradley needed to have in place for his longer-term well-being; we felt it was our responsibility as parents to address this before the time came when we couldn't care for him, or were no longer here to do so.

Autism is high-maintenance. It takes its toll on couples. Understanding this, my husband and I came up with a weekend camp program designed to give parents a break. The families of three students signed their kids up. On Friday, each brought a suitcase, and after school, they and their weekend staff drove to a small camp in Wisconsin, returning home to their parents on Sunday afternoon.

The success of the weekend camp led to an eight-week summer residential camp. Not all parents were comfortable with their children attending weekend or summer camps; how they intended to ease their autistic teens into an inevitable life without parents puzzled my husband and me. We probably were perceived as less "caring," but we're still here today fighting the fight, while other parents have departed without ever providing their autistic young person the chance to practice being in a new setting without them.

In the back of my mind, I knew the writing was on the wall: *"Brad must leave our home and get a home of his own."* I began to work on IDMH/DD with my ideas. There had never been a residential program for people with autism in Illinois. Roz was very much against it at the time. She absolutely refused to allow her son to be part of this, even if I were able to get it started.

In July 1979 my now 21-year-old son was in the first residential setting for adults with autism in Illinois, in a three-bedroom home. IDMH/DD funded psychiatrist Dr. Gregg Nunn for six months, so he could select and train the staff to provide Bradley with around-the-clock behavioral programs. We soon filled the remaining two residential openings. Thus was Rimland Residential inaugurated to supplement my son's day and working programs.

In 1980 I fell out of favor with Roz Oppenheim. My husband Bob no longer served as president of the Board of Directors at Rimland School. An observer from a speech and language clinic took note of the shocker, which had never been a secret; it was always in open view. This person reported that Bradley was treated "inhumanely." Aversives were not allowed in publicly funded behavior programs. The Board voted to take the shocker away from Brad's behavioral program, cold turkey. We were told that if we didn't comply, Bradley and the shocker could go in search of a different program.

Time and again, what we put in place to help our son seemed to end in his being "weeded out." Roz set up one behavior program for him after another. Each failed, at great expense to Brad's well-being. His negative behavior escalated because the "learning" was working in reverse. The steps put in place to contain Brad without the shocker merely fueled his confusion. The final program at Rimland had Brad's arms encased in huge plastic tubes. He couldn't bend his arms to hit his head with the tubes, being both heavy and tied down, but it meant he couldn't participate in any activity for which he could be positively reinforced.

Once again I approached the IDMH/DD in order to start another residential program for adults with autism, since my son was now excluded from the first one I'd started. With the help of Carol Ann Auclair, we put together a budget and did the necessary paperwork, presenting it to the Health Facility Planning Board. My husband and I worked with the Legislature, State Representatives, and Senators from both political parties—literally anyone who would listen. I spent a fortune, even hiring a lobbyist, to get a program started. My reasoning made Carol Ann laugh; my theory was that at Bradley's age, he would have by then charmed us out of a fortune for college, cars, vacations, and independence, had he been neurotypical. He was bone of our bone, and nothing would be denied him.

In 1981 I incorporated BLARE House (Better Living for Autistics in Residential Environments). Staff were hired to review the behaviors of Bradley and potential housemates, because behavioral programs needed to be in place before day one. Meanwhile, it took from July of 1981 until June of 1984 to finally locate and secure two homes in the Chicago suburbs, each for four clients. We managed to negotiate the necessary funding with IDMH/DD.

Bradley was the last of four clients to go into the Schaumburg, Illinois home. He was still managed at the time with the behavioral program that used the tubes to restrain his arms from head banging. At this point Roz started calling me frequently, ironically, to learn how soon Brad's bed in the Rimland Residential would be vacated; the death of her husband and her own illness were the only forces that could have moved her to seek residential placement for her son Ethan. Roz died soon after he was placed.

Brad's head banging challenged one behavior program after the other. As a last resort, he was tied to a wheel chair with a hood over his eyes; he would scream, and the pressure he applied to break his arm restraints caused his hands to swell. It was so horrible.

Bradley's doctor feared that his continued head banging would detach his retinas or aggravate the cataracts that had already formed, and that this would cause blindness. I approached IDMH/DD to request a reinstatement of the shocker as the historically least detrimental way to keep him from harm. They responded with a denial, and encouraged institutionalization. Under no circumstances would my husband and I allow him to be put in an institution.

Our son suffers from Neuroleptic Malignant Syndrome. He is also highly allergic. (We nearly lost him to a 107° temperature combined with a blood pressure of 250/150, from an allergic reaction.) We feared that a doctor in an institution would try to prevent head banging with restraints, or worse, with an injection that might cause a lethal allergic reaction.

What choice did we have, but to sue IDMH/DD? We hired Richard Friedman, an attorney who'd been head of HEW (Department of Health, Education, and Welfare) for five states during Nixon's administration. We also hired Dennis Olvera, Ph.D., to write a proper, humane program for Bradley. Dennis was the monitor for the Indiana Department of Mental Health, and had known Brad for years, commuting from his private practice in Indiana. We felt that Brad deserved this effort, after suffering the numerous stopgap measures over his young lifetime. We were in court five days a week for five months. ACLU was against us. Numerous parent groups as well as legal groups demonized me as the horrible, unfeeling mother who did not love her child, and even wanted to abuse him.

Bob O'Donnell, a lawyer (and later the father of a special needs child), joined with Richard Friedman and Dennis Olvera to make a fabulous team.

Together, they enabled Judge Stephen Yates to see us as loving parents who wanted the best for their only child. Judge Yates was appalled with the wheelchair/restraint program.

At this point, the state of Illinois made a decision to appoint a non-psychiatrist to head up IDMH/DD, but any decision to send Bradley to a state institution without a psychiatrist would be illegal, since medical decisions require psychiatric review. This legal technicality was the drastic mistake that caused them to lose the case. Bradley won!

At first it was difficult to renegotiate with an embarrassed IDMH/DD staff, who had to read about their costly faux pas in the Chicago newspapers. I pointed out to them that they didn't lose and we didn't win—only Bradley was the winner.

The judge made sure that Bradley wasn't abused. He was given one-on-one staff 24 hours a day, and every staff member was trained in the use of the shocker. The home was also monitored at each shift for pica material, as Brad had to have emergency surgery once, as a result of eating rubber gloves. Dr. Olvera headed up the program, trained the staff, and was hands-on. It was a perfect program, and Bradley thrived. He made tremendous strides. He began painting. BLARE House opened a small retail shop where he painted on silk. Our designers then placed his painted silk pieces on individual clothing—it was a big hit.

During this time, the Mayor of Chicago's wife, Maggie Daley, held a juried art show for people with any type of disability. Bradley submitted a hand-painted piece of silk that we framed. His work was chosen among others to be displayed in the Harold Washington Library.

The years have passed, and Bradley has progressed better than we could have imagined. He's still not verbal, but he almost never hits his head, and all in all seems like a happy man.

In 2003, after 17 years of funding Bradley's program, the State of Illinois decided to cut his funding down by two-thirds, with no explanation. Given that I'd retired from the Board of Directors of BLARE House, I turned to them to help get IDMH/DD to change their mind. BLARE House refused. The court consent decree stated that BLARE needed to negotiate with the IDMH/DD, but they refused. My husband and I offered to pay all legal fees that BLARE would incur, but they still refused. Before, these people would kiss my hands and tell me how wonderful I was to have made a place for their son or daughter, but now that they had services for their children, they wouldn't bother to help me, the person who'd helped them.

The State again wants my son to be institutionalized to cut costs. Bob and I decided to sue the Department of Health and Human Services for my son's treatment in the least restrictive environment as before, and we've also sued BLARE House for neglecting their fiduciary duty to Brad, and for not joining us in our effort to get proper treatment for him.

As of this writing, BLARE House has been taken over by Trinity Services. They too want him withdrawn from BLARE and put in an institution. We are his parents, and we will never let that happen.

This new lawsuit against BLARE House and Health and Human Services is just beginning. We must win. We will win. Our son's life is at stake. If he goes into an institution, he is certain to die.

THIRTY-FOUR

Dorothy Beavers

For many years after a massive heart attack, my husband had severe heart congestion. It was getting worse, and he had little energy, but still insisted that Leo come home every weekend from the group home where he lived. We compromised, so that every other week Leo spent the weekend at home, going out with his father to a restaurant. Leo didn't want me near his father and pushed me away constantly saying, "Go kitchen mommy" (because that's where he usually saw me).

My husband spoiled his son by giving him candy, pop, and all manner of junk food. We argued about filling Leo so full of fattening food, but I lost the argument. His father said, "Leo has few pleasures in his life and if he wants the stuff, I will give it to him. What difference does it make anyway?"

When Leo was 30, we felt we'd finally found a good place for him in a new local group home for 12 autistic adults. He was the only resident who had speech, because we'd taught him some before he went there.

When we thought he was settled in, my husband and I decided to go to the Caribbean to rest, since he was getting so weak he could hardly walk. He probably should have been on oxygen on the plane, but no one thought about it back then. I realized that he was in trouble when he started vomiting in the vacation condo. He was rushed to the St. Thomas hospital and stabilized overnight. After three weeks of recuperation in Miami, we flew back to Rochester. I decided to pick up Leo on the weekend, take him out to eat, and then take him to the hospital to visit with his father, who hadn't seen him for a month. I don't know why Leo didn't scream or yell as he usually did in a strange place; he was as good as an angel.

When we got to his father's room, I asked the nurse to put my husband in a chair so he could visit with his son. Leo came over to his father and started tugging at his hospital gown pleading, "Go get hamburger, go get hamburger." He never said, "Hi, daddy," or "I love you" as a normal person would—he was just frantic to get his father out of there. Since he was making so much noise and tugging on his father, I decided to take Leo home. I fixed our usual Friday supper of hot dogs and beans, gave Leo his bath and put him to bed, locking his bedroom door to keep him from wandering through the house at night. His father died that night.

The next time I took Leo home for the weekend, it was a sunny winter day and I thought I would take him out for lunch as his father had. I was trying to persuade Leo to go out with me. He was sitting on the sofa with his cars and stuffed animals when he suddenly hit me on the face and knocked me down. He cried and sobbed, "Want Daddy, want Daddy." After I recovered from the shock of his outburst, with both of us crying, I took him back to his group home. And throughout the many years since then, he has never hit me again or tried to hurt me.

Everyone has tried to explain to Leo that his father is dead and won't be coming back to see him anymore, but Leo doesn't understand. He still thinks, "Daddy's sick, Daddy's in hospital." How do you explain the concept of death to an autistic child? I still take Leo out once or twice a month, as I promised his father. And I fill Leo full of candy and pop and potato chips as his father did. "What difference does it make if Leo enjoys these things?" And I have to agree, if it's only once or twice a month it can't do that much harm.

The group home declines—Leo's rapes

The new group home at the school where Leo moved in 1990 seemed to be a wonderful place for him. The staff was very well trained, and there appeared to be good government funding. The supervisor of his home was a vibrant woman without children who had a sixth sense about how to run a group home with 12 autistic adults. As the years passed she went on to have a family, and left the unit. In 1995, a series of poor administrators without training appeared, just as New York State was reducing its funding.

The quality of the employees went downhill, and there were no more criminal checks. Leo's beautiful animal pictures on his bedroom walls, which had been specially made for him, disappeared. And when I brought him nice clothes, they were stolen within the week. (Daddy's shirt, which we both loved, was gone in a few days.)

The unit became rundown and dirty, and the autistic adults were beginning to look like bums because they weren't taken care of properly any more. Some employees slept on the job or were caught stealing. The morale was terrible and everything appeared to be in chaos. When Leo came home on weekends with me, he didn't want to go back to school, and fussed a lot as I drove him back.

There was talk of severe problems in the top administrative offices at the agency. The unit started fiddling with Leo's medications after his dad passed away, and he began to gain weight. Leo still looked very handsome when he was dressed up in a jacket or suit, but he was lethargic and slow.

I am a Ph.D. organic chemist with training in pharmacology and biochemistry. I looked at every one of Leo's meds and the doses he was taking. In one of Leo's annual reviews I pointed out to the staff that Leo was so over-medicated he was in a fog and acted like a zombie. I'd noticed that the staff doctor kept adding medication on medication without taking any away.

As the group home continued to go downhill, traumatic events began happening to Leo. I don't think the other autistic adults had such problems. I was called by the home with a report that Leo had crawled out his first floor window and the staff found him wandering alone on the front lawn with his stuffed animals, close to a well-traveled road. (He'd already been hit by a car once in the past.) Leo kept saying, "Go see Daddy, go see Daddy." (He hadn't said anything about Daddy in three years!) The home finally made the window secure so Leo couldn't crawl out again.

A week later, I was on vacation in California when the staff called saying that Leo had been badly beaten. Both eyes were purple-black, and his arms, face, and groin area were also black and blue. But most disturbing was the fact that Leo's genitals were black, and swollen and sore. I cried uncontrollably for the two days left in the tour. When I got home I rushed to see how Leo was doing. His bruises had begun to turn yellow and he appeared to be healing.

So my worst fears for Leo had finally come to pass; he'd been brutally raped or molested. The school downplayed it, saying that Leo had probably masturbated and caused the bruises himself. Leo did masturbate, but he never left a mark on his body, ever. This was a bona fide sexual attack! When Leo was asked how he got those bruises he answered, "Fall off balance beam," as if parroting someone's words. I imagine the rapist(s) had coached Leo to say that, since he didn't even know what a balance beam was.

For all of my son's life I'd feared that someone would molest him because he was good-looking, and he wouldn't be able to tell anyone what had happened to him. But the fact that he bruised easily (a family trait) had given the molester away. The group home called in the staff that worked with Leo and questioned them about Leo's bruises, but learned nothing. And so the incident was swept under the rug. It was reported to NYS authorities as required by law, but not a word was said to anyone, and it was kept secret.

I didn't tell any parents what had happened because I didn't want to frighten them. Thank God his father didn't live to see him in this condition.

Then it happened again four months later. A nurse called to say that Leo had been beaten *again*, even worse than before. I happened to be home this time and told the staff that I was coming down immediately. I insisted that Leo see the doctor and be examined *immediately*. The school nurse and I took him to a health clinic. The doctor examining Leo said that it appeared that he had been molested and "penetrated" since an exam of Leo's anus appeared to show bacteria that didn't normally grow there. Leo was taken to a rape crisis center in a hospital and his bruises photographed with a police camera (giving date and time). Poor Leo didn't know what was happening to him. We were at the rape crisis center for several hours and we didn't get to eat until 10:00 p.m. when they let us out of the hospital.

This time the agency really did try to catch the rapist(s), but no one was caught as far as I know. The school was so concerned that they decided to have only female staff take care of Leo, examining his body twice a day for bruises.

Each weekend when he came home I would check him for any unusual bruises on his body before I gave him his bath. For a few years he showed no signs of being molested, but then in 1999 *it started again*! Suspicious bruises and lots of fingerprints on his skin, in places where Leo couldn't reach. He gained 40 pounds during this time and his body became dumpy. Probably he was eating to calm his fears because of the molestation. I took pictures of the bruises under his arms, on his legs, and on his back. Circular bruises on his rear end were obvious and it looked like someone had hit him with a plunger. I took the pictures to a higher authority. The administrator said he would investigate, but if he did so, nothing was reported to me. I finally insisted that they call in the Attorney General of New York, Elliott Spitzer, since the agency's investigation got nowhere.

New York State investigators came and studied the group home for two months, looking at Leo's day-care unit and the residential setting. They finally stated that he had been molested, and that something had to be done about it *immediately.*

I don't know what the administrative staff did, but several more employees were let go in Leo's residence. And the suspicious bruising stopped! All this occurred while the group home and agency were getting into trouble; the newspapers had a field day. Several parents were interviewed by reporters. I was asked for an interview but refused; I didn't want to tell the world what had been going on with my son because the agency and group home might be shut down. Then where would the 12 autistic adults go for care? There was nothing available. I was asked by the home if I wanted to place Leo somewhere else. I said no, because there wasn't anyplace else! Everything that had happened to Leo in 1999 was hushed up again. The new staff knew nothing about Leo's molestation, until I told them.

Fortunately some real professionals and a new CEO worked hard to improve the agency. Leo's group home was cleaned up, and new staff added. Most of the new staff are kind, hard-working people who treat Leo well.

This experience taught me for the first time in my life that there really is good and evil in this world, and apparently always will be.

For the time being, the group home is back to its original fine condition, with good staff. But what will happen to Leo when I'm gone, with no one to protect him?

And if they ever find Leo's molester, I will tear him apart with my bare hands for harming my innocent, helpless son.

THIRTY-FIVE

Jim Cockey

Guilt and autism go hand in hand; while all parents make decisions they later regret, there can be especially dire consequences when a child has autism. This is the story of Israel, and how I struggled to rid myself, and my son, of our demons.

December 25, 2002 was the worst Christmas ever. Israel lay in bed all day long, ignoring the festivities. Periodically, his face grimaced involuntarily to one side, punctuated by an endless soft vocal tic.

A couple of months before, his dose of the anti-psychotic drug Zyprexa had been increased to the maximum that our psychiatrist deemed safe, 15 milligrams; in spite of what he'd been telling me, I knew on this particular Christmas day that I had to get Israel off Zyprexa.

It was not the first time I'd decided to take him off medication. Three years earlier I'd brought him home from the group home where he'd been living, with the idea of seeing if I could reduce his medication level. He was 22 years old and had been taking meds for about three years. As soon as we started reducing his Zyprexa, Israel began to show symptoms of tardive dyskinesia. When I saw those symptoms, knowing how serious such side effects could be, I knew I had to do my best to get him off drugs.

I'd agreed to start my son on medications at 19 because of self-aggression that started when he was nearly 12 years old. When he was 14 I took him to Salem, Oregon to work with Dr. Steve Edelson in a test group exploring Auditory Integration Training. Six months after that treatment, Israel's self-aggression dropped from 133 hits a day to zero. His life for the next few years was actually pretty good. He was living in a group home that was highly organized around the behavior modification principles of Ivar Lovaas, and he was well accepted in school. He was very skilled physically, but verbally limited. Although his demonstrated cognitive level seemed low, everyone working with him had the sense that he was in fact quite intelligent, but that his intelligence was somehow locked inside. He was mainstreamed in school with a one-on-one aide, with varying success. His sophomore year was spectacular; he ran in the cross-country team and recited lines in the plays that his drama class produced. He had an intelligent young aide whom he absolutely adored. During the summer he went to a fabulous camp in Ohio, called Camp Nuhop, where he developed what we came to call the "Camp Nuhop smile."

Then in the fall of 1996—after so many years of doing so well—Israel's self-aggression gradually returned. We expected that he might spontaneously improve, but he got worse and worse. But now Israel was physically strong enough to cause himself real harm. Given the same set of circumstances today I would never agree to put him on medication. But at that time, considering the only options I was aware of, I felt that I didn't have any choice. No decision has stoked the demon that feeds my guilt more profoundly than that one decision. No decision has caused me greater self-examination and growth.

Three years after starting Israel on medications, his stepmother Berni and I tried to get him off them. We'd just discovered the DAN! protocol, and were hoping that it would help ease the withdrawal. We also hoped that a month or two after getting off the medications he would start to improve. None of these hopes was realized.

We brought him home in June of 1999 and began decreasing the medications. Besides the Zyprexa, Israel was taking some Prozac and Propranolol. Getting him off the last two was actually pretty easy. By mid-November we started reducing the Zyprexa, and by mid-December things had deteriorated; his self-aggression returned with new vigor. He required one-on-one continuous supervision to prevent him from hitting himself. I lost about twenty pounds in the nine months that I worked with him at home. Everyone called it "Jim's weight-loss program." (The only problem was that I didn't need to lose weight.)

It was around the beginning of 2000 that Israel started biting his tongue. By the end of January he was medication-free, but he was also in a precarious state. He had to wear a sparring helmet to protect his head, and lip guards to protect his tongue. He and I were getting about two hours' sleep a night. In mid-February Israel's stepsister Ericka was diagnosed with a lymphoma, which turned out to be Hodgkin's disease. Our physical and emotional limits were exceeded. So only a month after getting off all his medications, he was put back on Zyprexa and sent back to his group home. My line for describing that year was, "We came, we saw, and we got the hell out of there."

I felt defeated and depressed. I composed a string trio entitled *Elegy to an Ancient Battlefield* right after Israel left our house. The title alludes to the *Iliad*, but it's a metaphor for the battle we'd just endured. By May Israel was stable in his new living environment, and Ericka was without her beautiful hair, but well on the way to recovery. It seemed to me in those days that one of our children had been sacrificed to the cosmos, and another one had been saved.

Back to that horrible Christmas of 2002: I decided that I couldn't stand by and watch my kid go down. I knew that we were all going to have to go back to the battlefield to get Israel off his medications, and that this time we had to succeed. We'd all learned a lot during that first attempt, and I realized that if we hadn't tried and failed the first time, we wouldn't succeed the second time.

This is the first lesson: "failure" is the source of new information. I realized that we needed to reverse the order of the medication withdrawal. In 1999–2000, we'd taken Israel off the easy ones first, leaving him no medication support when he came off the most powerful drug. So instead, in 2003 we took Israel off Zyprexa (the most profound and difficult medication) first. That way he still had the Prozac and Trazodone to cushion the neurological shock of being without Zyprexa.

Second, we had to let Israel show us the way. In 1999–2000 we still had Behavior Modification thinking, which made us think we knew what was best for Israel. Our modus operandi for 2003 was to trust him implicitly. It was imperative that everyone working with him understood that he was trying his best, and that he knew what he was capable of handling and what he needed.

Third, I had to take hold of and understand the role of parent: the only person who might hold the child's best interests at the center. Everyone else, including educators, therapists, care providers and medical profession-als has another agenda, no matter how good a person or how accomplished they might be in their profession. The parent is the only one whose agenda might be purely in the interest of the child, so it's the parent who must trust intuition and take control of the program.

There was a fourth factor involved, but I'm not sure what to call it—fate, luck, divine intervention, or the way of the universe. Doors hidden in 1999 revealed themselves in 2003, and phone calls that hadn't helped in 1999 gave us valuable information now. There is something about timing, and something about sensing when things are working. A phone call to Dr. Bernard Rimland put us in touch with Dr. Alan Lewis, who after 45 minutes on the phone with me said, "Your son is constipated. Give him a supposi-tory treatment for three days." This treatment was one of the main reasons we were able to get Israel off Zyprexa. Through Dr. Steve Edelson, I con-tacted Sharon Lee of the Oregon Autism Society. She got us started using TEACCH, a picture-based program developed over the last 35 years at the University of North Carolina. Israel's group home embraced this approach, and it helped him a lot.

I had to hold my ground when we got to the final stages of getting off Zyprexa. Israel's self-aggression abated for a month after the suppository treatment, but became a concern again as we approached the end-date of his Zyprexa. Everyone was concerned, but I knew we could do it, and that we had to do it. The folks at Israel's group home did what they could to convince me to stop reducing his medications. There were a few tense meetings when I was the only person on Israel's support team who felt we should continue with the withdrawal. I held my ground, and we succeeded.

By March 1, 2003, Israel was completely off Zyprexa.

I think the most profound insight, which was to guide us through the next two years of complete withdrawal from medications, was the discov-ery that Israel really does know his needs. Our role was to support him through his own discoveries of self-management and recovery.

In the beginning, Israel coped with being off Zyprexa by withdrawing. He would stay in his room for days, and indoors for weeks. He would burrow under a mountain of bedcovers all day long, only leaving his room to go to the bathroom. He would even eat in his bed. In keeping with our new approach, we didn't try to get him out of his room, as we would have done in the past. (On rare occasions, we would change this policy, and encourage him to leave his room. But those times were extremely rare, and only upon very, very careful consideration.) Most of the time, the rule was *What Israel Wants, Israel Gets.*

A tremendous amount of patience and trust was required. There was about a six-week period when Israel didn't go outside once. Then, in May of 2003, he went outside and sat on a bench for about 15 minutes, a huge event. On June 24, 2003, he took a half-mile walk. It took him four and a half hours. He draped his head and body with blankets and pillows for security. He'd walk a few steps, then stoop down and finger the dirt for 15 to 30 minutes. Then he'd get up and walk a few more paces. This brave venture into the world was a major milestone. By the end of the summer he was taking short hikes.

During that summer, Israel worked with a psychologist schooled in Relationship Development Integration therapy (RDI). This amazing work nurtured his innate personality traits of love and humor. I will never forget the day that Israel looked at me and said, "I want my Dad," or the day that he laughed because the psychologist, Dr. Tyler Whitney, was gently teasing him in a humorous and friendly way. In his 26 years Israel had never expressed longing for another human, and only once before, his first day at Camp Nuhop, had he laughed a real, heartfelt laugh. RDI facilitated Israel's search for Israel.

He didn't escape medication without some lingering side effects. On the very day that Israel came completely off Zyprexa, a vocal tic that'd been very, very soft suddenly became a yell. This Tourette's-like yell continued without stop for six months. Then in September it gradually became less, and even stopped for a few weeks. But it came back, and still persists on a daily basis, although to a less frequent and generally less intense level than during those first few months.

Israel started biofeedback that fall. It was after his first session that his vocal tics stopped for longer than three minutes. Further treatments have had periodic success. Around this time he also began sensory integration therapy. He spent countless hours completely buried in a big box filled with plastic balls. His vocal tics often stopped during these sessions.

All of these experiences set the stage for 2004, when Israel's life changed profoundly. This new direction began with our trip to Seattle, Washington to visit the HANDLE Institute. It felt completely different from any other therapy, as if we were beginning to touch on the real thing. HANDLE techniques are very similar to sensory integration therapy, but different. The practitioners get immediate responses from their clients that no one else can, and Israel was no exception. He seemed like a different person when we were there.

February, March, April, May, and June 2003 Israel's life was filled with HANDLE, TEACCH, sensory integrative therapy, RDI, and biofeedback. He was also on massive amounts of nutritional supplements and still following the casein- and gluten-free diet of the DAN! protocol, which we'd started in 1999. He was still on Prozac and Trazodone. Self-aggression, sometimes very, very hard, was still an issue, but between staff support, protective towels, hats, and pillows, and occasional increases of medication, Israel was getting through fairly well.

In May of 2004, when I was browsing the internet looking for a craniosacral therapist, my search led me to the website of Dr. Lewis Mehl-Madrona, a medical doctor and alternative-medicine practitioner. He is also a Lakota shaman. His website described weeklong intensive therapy sessions in which therapists work under his supervision, using a wide variety of modalities. I called Dr. Mehl-Madrona and he immediately agreed to schedule a week with Israel.

In July 2004 we went to Tucson, Arizona along with Israel's Aunt Tara, for ten days of intensive therapy. It was a life-changing experience for both Israel and me. It set us on a course that we still follow, and which has enriched our lives. It showed me that we could save my son's quality of life, and it showed me the path to follow: one of trust, intuition, research, honesty, endurance, patience, and optimism. Dr. Mehl-Madrona's first book, *Coyote Medicine*, outlines the whole path. Everything Israel and I have done since our time in Tucson is based on those foundations. The last paragraph of the book says it all: *Don't give up. Ever.*

We worked with a lot of healers in Tucson, and I suspect they all did some good. The acupressure therapy seemed to have the most immediate effect, and by the end of the ten days, he removed the hat that he'd worn for three years. We saw smiles we hadn't seen for years. One of the most profound experiences was the Native American "sweat" that we did with Dr. Mehl-Madrona and some of the other folks who were there. It took a lot of bravery on Israel's part to do the sweat, and it seemed to transform him. After the sweat he and I lay on the ground outside of the sweat lodge and just looked at the stars for half an hour. There was a peacefulness about Israel that night.

I made a huge decision during that trip: to take Israel out of the group home and move him to our own second home in Boise, Idaho, where we would continue this kind of therapy. It was a radical decision that affected not only Israel and me but almost everyone associated with me, especially my family. In the two years since, Israel has been through many therapies and therapists; craniosacral therapy, acupuncture, acupressure, Alexander Technique, Chi Gong, $E=MC^2$, psychic therapy, chakra balancing, magnetic work with Dr. William H. Philpott, Sacred Circles, RDI, Dr. Andrew Weil's tape about breathing, EarthPulse (electromagnetic sleep aid), Chinese herbs, Ayurvedic diet, prism eyeglasses, colored eyeglasses, rotation diet, and nutritional supplements such as Equilib. Recently he's worked with neurofeedback and NAET (allergy elimination), combined with other modalities, especially enzyme therapy and the work of Dietrich Klinghardt, MD, Ph.D. Israel has now been off medication for a year and a half, and continues to improve. Most recently, that improvement has been profound.

When we first returned from Tucson, I followed that model of intensive therapy. I wasn't as concerned about knowing which therapies were effective as I was that progress was being made. I was also aware that the synergy of combined effects could be powerful. I eventually reduced the number of therapies so I could get a better sense of which were showing the most positive results. Now we pretty much work with one therapist at a time. Some therapies take a long time to integrate and some have lasting effects, so there will always be an element of uncertainty as to which is the most effective.

The search for answers changes the searcher. When I took Israel to Tucson for therapy I was given therapy right along with him. At first I rejected this concept; so far as I was concerned it was all about him, and I didn't want the focus or the energy to dissipate. Gradually I started to accept that the need for me to get therapy was not only for me, but also for Israel. If I were healthier, and not fighting things like guilt, I would be a more effective researcher and decision-maker. Then I began to entertain the thought that there was an even more profound reason: I began to see that we were connected, as all parents and children are connected, not only genetically and through environment, but also because of more subtle bonds. Because of these subtle bonds, personal strides made by one individual can affect the other person. These simultaneous strides might seem unrelated, but they occur to a significant extent.

I've found that a certain therapy might not work at one time, but a year or two down the road it might have profound effects. A therapy should not be discounted just because it doesn't work the first time. Our work with NAET in 2000 seemed to have no efficacy; this year, it seems to be having a very great effect.

In January of 2006 Israel started having seizures, or perhaps panic attacks (there is debate on this issue). My research led me to Margaret Ayers, and her work with neuro-feedback. In March we went to Los Angeles for two weeks and did daily work with Ms. Ayers that seemed to help a lot. In April we started work with Stephanie Kennedy, who does the NAET and digestive health work. In January Israel was having seven to fourteen seizures a week, now he has between one and four.

Israel's had erratic sleep patterns. A few years ago we noticed he'd do surprisingly better with less sleep; the day following a sleepless night was quite often a great one in terms of mood, behavior, and vocal tics. In October of 2004, with the help of the EarthPulse magnet sleep aid, his sleep stabilized considerably, and a 48-hour cycle became apparent. One day of the cycle was easy for Israel to handle and the other was difficult. The cycle is still apparent, but his ability to handle it has improved dramatically. Recently, we've seen very few days when substantial protection or security support is needed.

Israel now lives in his own home with a 24-hour staff. He's been blessed with a trust fund sufficient for his needs. A house manager and I manage his home. My son is fortunate to have this living arrangement. He used to live in a good group home setting, but his life was degenerating. Now it's filled with hope and promise, thanks to all we've learned.

Most of the literature about autism is focused on young children because this is where there's the most potential for improvement, and there is an apparent epidemic of new cases. But what about the adults? Israel's story shows that there's room for profound improvement in adulthood, even when the challenges seem overwhelming. Neurologists keep extending the time frame that they consider the brain to be neuroplastic, to be able to grow and change. Certain therapies, especially in alternative medicine, can have far-reaching effects on adults as well as children. Yet the field perseverates on the children—where are the adults? And how are they doing? And what helps them?

It's my hope that our story will enlighten some who read it about the dangers of medication, and point to the many viable alternatives. I'd like to think that our story can give some hope and guidance to anyone struggling to improve the lives of the autistic adults they care for.

Israel is showing more interest in his environment than he has for many years. He acknowledges people more, and he explores his house more. He willingly does chores and is doing things he was never interested in doing before, like fixing dinner or entering marks in the logbook. We now see many happy days in a row. If this continues, next Christmas might well be the best Christmas ever.

THIRTY-SIX

Audrey Flack

Years ago, Dr. Bernard Rimland (Director and founder of the Autism Research Institute) asked me to contribute a chapter to a book tentatively titled *A Better Life for Autistic Adults: Lessons Learned by Parents Who Have Been There*. I didn't respond, in spite of the fact that I have the highest regard for Bernard Rimland, and have been "there" ten times over. I assumed stories of hope and success were the idea, and felt I didn't have anything to contribute; as a matter of fact, I was annoyed by the whole idea. There are those of us (I suspect large numbers) who don't have many stories of hope or success, and some who don't have any at all. I thought a lot about it and discussed it with my husband. We couldn't come up with even one such story.

Yet I'm responding years later to a second request because my autistic daughter has become a miracle and a source of joy, even though she remains severely autistic. I think her story is worth telling. It doesn't fit the prescribed category, but I believe there is much to be learned from her journey.

Melissa was born at a time when the incidence of autism was one in ten thousand. My child was the one. It was also a time when mothers were blamed for their child's condition. It was implied that we wanted to injure our children, that we even wanted them dead. I was called a "Refrigerator Mother," a cold, heartless, and rejecting person. Nothing could be further from the truth. This theory of causation was a fabrication from the distorted mind of a Dr. Bruno Bettelheim, who years later apologized, and also committed suicide, acts which could neither erase nor redeem the many years when the entire medical establishment mindlessly endorsed his teachings. He was lauded and rewarded, while we mothers were condemned and berated. Meanwhile our children received no help from the psychological pseudo-theories that were based on Bettelheim's outrageous premise.

Years later I came across *Infantile Autism* by Dr. Bernard Rimland and gained a better understanding of the workings of the autistic mind. Dr. Rimland debunked the blaming psychological theory, and was the first person to ascribe the mysterious condition to physical causes. As a result, Melissa began to receive some understanding and a bit of treatment, and I felt redeemed, although the years of guilt remain embedded in the deepest part of me. Bernard Rimland will forever be my hero, as well as a hero to the entire autistic community.

Melissa is 47 years old now, and she still can't speak. She tries hard, holding my cheeks and looking into my eyes, but what comes out are repetitive sounds like "bugga bugga bugga" or "monga monga monga." There are distinct thoughts in her head, questions she wants to ask, things she wants to know, and feelings she wants to express, but she is bound by crossed "wires" and bent dendritic connections.

In the beginning, she railed with frustration, destroying everything in sight, her agony and anger so great that the family collapsed under the weight of her autism. She couldn't write or even point to an object. She had no way to express herself other than "stimming," throwing herself onto the floor and having a tantrum, or decimating the house.

She would shove food into her mouth and swallow it with such speed and desperation I thought she might choke. I could not take my eyes off her for one second—literally not one second. On the occasions I took Melissa and her younger sister, Hannah, out to eat, she bit off the tips of plastic forks and swallowed them. I learned to bring my own metal utensils.

Finding a bathroom in time was usually traumatic. Accidents abounded. She snatched food from other people's plates in restaurants with a speed that exceeded comprehension. She did this while walking to our table, looking straight ahead. Her peripheral vision is uncanny. Her memory is uncanny. She did not sleep for four years and went around the apartment going full speed ahead, sometimes with a knife in her mouth. I didn't have the heart to tie her to her bed, so I followed her around for four years and wound up looking like a concentration camp victim.

In spite of this devastation and disruption, Melissa has transformed herself into the most amazing and beautiful human being I have ever known. She is an angel on earth, and I will try to offer some thoughts on how this came about. The process was slow and only happened with time and persistence. There were no immediate solutions to specific problems, no short cuts.

There were many times when we thought she didn't understand what we asked of her. It took a while for us to realize that she needed time to process words. Sometimes she needed five minutes, sometimes she needed hours, sometimes weeks, and sometimes years. With a secure, stable environment in a wonderful school we found for her, she's become able to deal with her own processing system. So as someone who has been "there," I can say that *time, patience,* and *kindness* are the keys. Autism cannot be rushed. The changes in Melissa have come about over years, and they are worth the effort.

There is one experience I would like to share here which might be of great help to parents whose child has to be hospitalized.

Melissa loves baths. She loves to loll in the water and is fascinated as it rushes from the faucet. She can stare at it for hours without blinking. She becomes transfixed—she cocks her head to the side and smiles, transported into an autistic world of pleasure. Who knows what visions she sees? I know that when I begin to see with Melissa's eyes, the world becomes magical. Sitting with her, perhaps following the path of a raindrop as it winds its way down a windowpane, takes me out of profane time and carries me into the sacred world of timelessness. This is the world that Melissa inhabits. There are no deadlines, no ego considerations, and no need for power or wealth.

Ironically, Melissa made enough progress that one day she decided to give herself a bath without anyone knowing it. She got into the bathtub and turned on the faucet; it was the hot water faucet, and it poured down on her feet. She didn't or couldn't get herself out. I suspect she froze. By the time someone got to her, her feet were severely burned.

Melissa was rushed to the burn ward of the hospital in excruciating pain. She wailed like an animal, curled up in a fetal position, and shut down. She would not eat or drink; these are serious problems for burn victims. The body needs proteins to repair itself and hydration is a must, but she wouldn't open her mouth. Ever since she was a child, she wouldn't drink water, and made a terrible face when it was offered to her. The hospital staff found this hard to understand even after I explained it to them. There was no recourse but intravenous hydration, but the nurses couldn't locate her veins because she has a delicate body and her veins are small. The nurses poked and prodded and finally resorted to putting a needle in her groin. She had to be restrained from pulling it out; her hands were tied to the railing of her bed. My husband tried to calm me, but I was beside myself.

Attending doctors came around, but kept their distance. They stood at the foot of her bed as if they were afraid of her—afraid of my poor helpless child. They did not take her hand or move close to her or really talk to her—their speech was stiff and spoken as if from a distance.

I explained that she was autistic, that she could understand but could not speak, but it did no good. They'd never treated an autistic person before. It's ironic that these doctors themselves behaved like autistic people: talking over my head, not making eye contact, looking the other way, not communicating.

I was frantic. My child needed help and proper nutrition. They couldn't keep sticking needles in her and walking away. A week went by and I feared for her life. I had the same helpless feeling I had during the "Refrigerator Mother" days when Melissa was young and the doctors treated me as if I were a disturbed neurotic. I called a psychotherapist friend in New York to talk about the situation. She advised me to call for a meeting of the entire staff assigned to her case to discuss the best way to handle Melissa and her treatment. She asked if there was a psychologist or social worker on the staff, but there was none.

I knew she was right. Her support and direction empowered me, and I went to the head nurse and demanded a summit meeting. My intent was strong, so I took control—I was angry.

It took that kind of gritty determination—the same determination young parents must exert when looking for school programs for their children—only this had to be accomplished immediately. It was imperative that the staff understand Melissa in order to help her. The meeting took place the next day in the hospital conference room, with doctors, nurses, my husband, and me. I talked about autism, described Melissa, told them how they needed to approach her, to speak to her, and they listened.

"She is a human being. She picks up your feelings and she is terrified. You have to talk softly to her, move slowly, and stand closer than the foot of her bed. Hold her hand, relate to her—she feels, she understands!"

It worked. She drank sodas and apple juice and began to respond and to watch TV. Melissa got better.

So the advice I would give if you ever get into such a fix is to realize that people, even doctors if they've never experienced autism first hand, tend to feel afraid when they're dealing with the unfamiliar. The fear makes them keep a distance, and it can affect their judgment and derail proper medical treatment. Do not lose your temper, but be strong and firm and explain in detail what is expected of them. Tell them how they should act toward your beautiful child.

What's become of Melissa

Melissa has adjusted. The rage and frustration of years ago have all but disappeared. She still tries to communicate. We look into each other's eyes, and our faces touch. I try to fathom her thoughts and guess at what she is trying to say. Sometimes I succeed. When I do, she claps her hands to let me know. Sometimes I can't figure it out and we're both stymied. I feel so bad as I sense her pain. A pensive look creeps over her delicate and beautiful face but the moment quickly passes and she goes on to the next thing in her life—looking at a leaf moved by the breeze, or following a rivulet of rain running down a car window, watching the dancing patterns of flickering light on the pavement, or studying the topology of a piece of curled paper.

She turns her head toward me and offers a forgiving smile, grateful for the slightest pleasure. Missy has become an angel. She's chosen to communicate with smiles. She has chosen to laugh. She's taught me how to love, how to be grateful for everything, how to accept the human condition.

Melissa has become pure love. She's emerged from the darkness and panic to become the extraordinary person she is. Her radiant beauty makes you feel better. She's at a wonderful school, Melmark, in Pennsylvania, and the other people who live there do for my heart and soul good too. It's as if you could condense the liquid from several pounds of grapes until you're left with one intensely concentrated drop. And that drop contains the essence of love, unmarked, with no agendas, no expectations. It radiates to all those around it, and the ones who see it or feel it are lucky enough to get a taste, and they are changed forever.